Cracks in the Potter's Clay

How I Overcame Bipolar I with Faith

Pastor Allison Joan Hall

Love,

Allison

Cracks in the Potter's Clay
Copyright 2021 by Allison Joan Hall
ALL RIGHTS RESERVED

Publisher: Absolute Author Publishing House
Editor: Doris Dobson
Cover Designer: Gabriel Delgado

ISBN Paberback: 978-1-64953-245-9
ISBN eBook: 978-1-64953-241-1

Dedication

I dedicate this book to my mother, the late Rev. Dr. Joan Gross Coursey. All that I am is because she was. She was a dancer, actress, teacher, wife, mother and lover of God. Through her example, I became everything that she was. When God told me that He was going to take her home on my 29th birthday, I asked Him if He could give me a double portion of my mother's anointing. Two years ago, I began to surrender everything to God and I believe He answered my prayer. Through the power of the Holy Spirit, I walk in the victory every day. I am grateful for the love my mother poured into me and the example she set for me.

Acknowledgments

I would like to acknowledge Yahweh foremost for creating me and saving my soul and granting me peace. I thank Him for sending His son Yahshua and for the Holy Spirit.

These people are people that I have been close with and whom I love and appreciate for adding to my life, for supporting me and for making me grow. If you do not see your name here, look in my prayers that follow and if you do not see it there, as my former Pastor and dear friend of my mother, Rev. Dr. Peggy Wall says; "Blame it on the head, not the heart."

The late Isaiah and Rebecca Johnson, The late Rev. Joan Gross Coursey, Ahmed Abdukarim, Adrienne Townes, Douglas Hall, Joshua Hall, Christina Hall, Gabriel (Charlie) Delgado, Kameha Delgado, Andre Pridgen, Deanna Pridgen, Audrey Hall, Tracey Hall, the late Ruth Gross, the late Charles Gross Jr., Kevin Gross, Michael (Macky) Gross, Dwayne Gross, Charles Gross III, Charlene (Dime) and Winston

Williams, Colleen Gross, Isaiah and Theresa Johnson, the late Samuel and Glaldys Mitchell, the late Victoria Mitchell, the late Ruth MacMurray, the late Alphonso and Naomi Wiggins, Edythe and Ronald Jones, LaShelle Allen, the late Josephine Murray, Judith Kitz, Amina Wolf, Omar Abdulkarim, Hassan Abdulkarim, Ali Abdulkarim, Amna, Jen, Jasmine, Jackson, Anisah, Layla, Isaiah, Aliyah, Angela Gray, Joseph Gray, Patricia Gray, Dougie Brown, LaToya Brown Clark, Marion Queensbury-Griner, Isabella, Jeannie Comparini, Dr. Edward Bryant Jr., Heather Tate, Steven Tate, Charlynn Gross, Michael (Mike-Mike) Gross, Kevin Gross, the late Thelma Smith, the late Mona Smith, Teddy Smith, Thelma Smith, Eunice Johnson, Peggy Williams, Tyrone Smith, Timmy Smith, Terry Smith, Thaliya Cruz, Carmen Baggett, Sheila Cross, Doris Dobson, Joyce and Nathaniel Batty, JoAnn House, Leon White, Eunice Johnson, Veda Moore, Angela Smith, Tamara Payne, Patti Owens, Byron Murphy, the late Viola Procise, the late Bertha Procise, the late Hattie Hall, Nancy Hall, Semone Hall, Doc and Pam Tisdale, Trudi McCullough, Nate Daily, Alexis Dillard, Rico Rivera, Andre Cooper, Shy Miles, Waverly Miles, Dr. Missy Patrylo, Dr. Don Teubner Rhodes, Yulanda Tisdale, William Sanders, Sandra Wright-Short, Charlotte Baker, Junius Jones, Kellee Gonzales, Annie Leshon, Reginald Stroud, Regina O'Neal, Garrett Hardy, Ian, Clarrie, William, George

Plakosh, Alice Eskins, Remus Medley, Keith and Penny Birkhead, the late Michelle Melton, Maria Marinakis, Jennie Boisseau, Courtney White, Gwendolyn Rohart, Les Brown, Jon Talarico, Mary Freeman, Eva Gorman, Todd Gray, Rosita, Mildred, Shirley, Kendra, Emma and Ernest Cross, Chinetta, Sandy, Tanya, Yuvisela, Grace, Maria Taylor, Latoya, Trina, Tony Holston, Joy, Colleen, Ron, Marina, Miluska, Wary, Silvia, Erma, Lizzie, Alonzo, Jennifer Simmons, Ellen Logan, Evelyn Freeman, Teniecka Drake, Gloria, Lydia, Isis, Ify, Precious, Yashica, Daliesha,   Dave, Michelle, Joe, Judy, Kelechi, Kathleen, Evelyn, Shanica, Mary, Etienne, Todd Rasnake, Andre Cooper, Leon White, Wendy, Muhammad, Kevin Knowlin and Alvester Jacobs.

Ministers who influenced me during my wilderness experience:

Peggy Wall, Gary Johnson, D'Artegnon Tisdale, Jameliah Gooden, Trudi McCullough, TD Jakes, Sharon Rich, Cheryl Strickland, Tammy Lyde, Charlotte Baker, Valerie Howard-Jones, Sheila Wright, Rodney Booth, Priscilla Shirer, Tony Evans, Robert Morris, Les Brown, Jon Talarico, Marsha Brown, Domenika Ringold, Emma Barnes, Debra Watkins, William McMillan, Marcus Rogers, Karen Wheaton, Dale Bronner, Trent Shelton, Trina

Mashell, Crys Speaks, Reginald Kennedy, Barry Rodemaker, Jermisha McCray, Creflo Dollar, Joyce Meyer, Joel Osteen, Tyler Perry, Steve Harvey, Kynan Bridges, Denzel Washington, Steven Furtick, Jentezen Franklin, Joseph Prince, Tauren Wells, Danny Gokey and Alex and Stephen Kendrick.

TABLE OF CONTENTS

Forward

Allison was a student in my Power Voice Academy. I had the pleasure of listening to her story. I developed the Power Voice Academy to inspire others to be "hungry" and to use their stories to inspire others. I had heard Allison for years, but I never took it apart the way she did. She said that there are two ways to spell Allison, but her late mother spelled her name A-l-l i-s o-n. That spells "All is on," and that is how she lives her life. She does not let anything stop her. Witnessing her bubbly personality and captivating smile, it was surprising to hear that she has been married and divorced three times and that she had been suffering from Bipolar 1. She took medicine for 20 years and has been medication -free for over a year now. She says that I had a big influence in her life listening to me speak at the Georgia Dome in front of 80,000 people. Now, she speaks daily on Facebook on what she calls her prayer run. She runs with her dog and prays for people as they tune in. She also speaks daily on YouTube in which she sings hymns, reads the Bible, and prays. She says that she prays and speaks from the heart as I do. She also sent me videos of her dancing liturgically. It is hard to believe that she is 55 years old. She is robbing the grave of her dreams.

Her book is very inspirational and informative. I absolutely love her transparency. Allison is a retired Spanish and Art teacher. She had a successful 22-year career until she was forced to retire due to health issues associated with some medication she was taking. Now she is off medication and is winning in life. She said life is not over until she wins. She has created a legacy for her two children and granddaughter by writing this book but has posted more than 698 inspirational posts on YouTube, Facebook, and Instagram since June 7, 2019. She says her ability to post to inspire people is her continued testimony of God's goodness and faithfulness. She says there used to be times when she would be depressed for weeks at a time. The videos are her proof that Bipolar 1 is beatable. She kicks its butt every day that God wakes her up.

All is on has not only included her secrets to managing the symptoms of Bipolar 1 but has shared what she has learned about creating Airbnb's and healthy eating. It has been a pleasure watching Allison develop her story. I have selected her to be one of the speakers at my final Power Voice Summit on June 5, 2021. She was selected out of thousands of participants. I am proud that she is a part of my legacy.

Les Brown

Introduction: Are You Playing The Potter?

Have you ever heard the term: Stay in your lane? Literally, it is imperative that, during a track event, the runner stays in his or her own lane. If they cross the line, they are disqualified. I love running track and I always stay in my lane. But in the track meet of life, I was supposed to be running in lane one and I crossed all the way over to lane six. I disqualified myself multiple times...in God's eyes that is.

Jeremiah 18:4 But the pot he was shaping from the clay was marred in his hands; so, the potter formed it into another pot, shaping it as seemed best to him. This foundational text above can be found in the Bible, but it is not just a Christian notion. It is universally true. We did not create ourselves. The potter is the Creator. He put the exact mixture of ingredients together in order to form us with all our uniqueness. Not even twins have the same fingerprints. Consider all the different textures and colors of hair people have, curly red hair, straight red hair, bushy hair, stringy hair, blonde hair, black hair, and brown hair. Even within the different races there is a variety of skin colors. Some of us have freckles and some of us do not. Some of us are tall and some of us are short. Our voices are even unique to us. When a potter creates something with his hands, every piece is different because it is made by hand. God is the Potter.

A potter does not sit down at the wheel until he has an idea of what he wants to create. He creates with a purpose in mind. I speak this from experience. While majoring in Fine Art (Studio Art Concentration) at Christopher Newport University, I took a wheel throwing class. Before my instructor gave me the clay to work with, I had to come up with a design and that design had to be both appealing to the eye and useful for the receiver. At the time, I was a smoker, and I chose to create an ashtray. The ashtray had a purpose. It was to catch ashes and to prevent fires. Cigarettes would burn safely in the ashtray. The ash tray had a purpose. Nothing is created without a purpose.

Cracks in the Potter's Clay

There is a quote by Steve Bow who was the president of the Metropolitan Life Insurance company that I absolutely love. It states: God's gift (the Potter) to us (the clay) is more talent and ability than we will ever hope to use in our lifetime. Our gift to God is to develop as much of that talent and ability as we can in this lifetime. We are so much more useful than an ashtray or a pot. Revelations 4:11 Worthy are You, our Lord and our God, to receive glory and honor and power; for You created all things, and because of Your will, they existed and were created. Even the tiny creation, the bee has its purpose in making honey. The honeybee colony makes 60 pounds of honey a year. Man's mind is so much more complex than a bee's but fulfilling his purpose is not as easy as making honey. Man can send a rocket to the moon and build a box named Alexa that can answer practically any question that it is asked within seconds. But man's mind can also be very troubled.

I was diagnosed with Bipolar 1 in 1999 and I took medicine for it for close to twenty years. One characteristic of Bipolar 1 is having an excessive amount of energy while requiring extraordinarily little sleep. I used to use my energy to try to be the potter and the clay. Not just the potter of my life but the potter of other people's lives also. I thought it was my job to make sure everyone else was happy. The more I did for other people, especially my family, the more fulfilled I felt. I thought that it was my job to keep everyone happy and comfortable. This caused me all kinds of relationship problems. You see, I expected to be appreciated and not to be taken for granted. I would get upset when I was not treated the way I treated others.

I was trying to be the Potter. I felt that since I created experiences for people to be happy, I was to be praised for that or at least appreciated. Wow. I cannot believe I just confessed that. One classic symptom Bipolar 1 people have is a delusion of grandeur. I had the answers. I knew how to think in order to make things happen. I thought positively. I had the stick-to-itiveness and the energy to get things done. I noticed that no one around me had the same level of energy that I had. It was only when I became isolated from all my immediate family did I begin to see the errors of my ways. I thought I was the Potter. The real Potter had to have a conversation with me. I could not hear Him with anyone else around. Once alone with Him, He shared secrets with me to true peace of mind, body and soul.

Cracks in the Potter's Clay

I am a confessed Believer in the Holy Trinity; God the Father, God the Son and God the Holy Spirit. Only recently, have I learned how to access the power of the Holy Spirit and my life has changed for the better. I walk in victory every day. No more depressive episodes lasting weeks. No more uncontrolled rantings, ravings and fights. You do not have to be a Christian to benefit from what I have learned. I am writing this book to help all people; not just those suffering from Bipolar 1. I am not a doctor. I am not making any guarantees of results. I don't play the Potter any longer. I am the clay; the vessel. I am not in charge of my life anymore. I give Him total control now and He leads me. I walk in the victory every day. If I can, you can too.

Part I

Chapter 1: The Surface

I had heard about God by attending church with my grandmother as a child. My maternal grandparents were Jewish, known as Hebrew Israelites. They worshipped on Saturdays and it was an all-day event. Lunch time was the best part of the day for me. The Church of God and Saints of Christ had the best cooks in the world. (I believe they still do.) I even remember traveling to Belleville, VA for one Passover and the food was delicious there too. I heard the word God, but I did not really understand the concept. My first experience with God happened when I was 6 or 7 years old.

Even though my mother sent us to church with my grandmother as a child, she did not go to church regularly herself back then. I do, however, recall her taking us to church on a few Easter Sundays. I remember getting new outfits with hats and posing for pictures. This Easter Sunday, we went to a church on Liberty Heights Avenue not far from our house. They had an Easter Egg Hunt. I remember the church building being made of big black stones. I remember walking towards the back of the church where no other children were looking for eggs. I remember kneeling down on the grass to pick up a pink coloured egg and I noticed how green the grass looked. Then I looked around at the flowers before me. My eyes then looked up at the blue sky with the white puffy clouds. I had a feeling that I had never felt before. It was calm and warm. I remember saying out loud: "Ohhhhhhh, you're God." I felt His presence in nature.

He was always with me. I was a very petite child and small for my age until I reached middle school. I used to love to climb into small places and hide. One summer day in Ocean Pines, MD, where we had a summer home, my sister Adrienne came up with the great idea to play magic act with a footlocker. She played the role of the magician and I was the assistant. She proceeded to lock me in the chest. She had a sense of humour, so she jokingly told me that she could not get the lock open. When I started to panic, she relieved me that she was only joking. Well, I was waiting for her to open the locker to let me out and it was not happening. I was locked inside.

3

I had to persuade Adrienne to go and get my mother for help because she did not want to upset my mother that she had locked me in a chest. Our mother was extremely dramatic. I remember hearing Adrienne talking to her in the other room. I heard just what I expected to hear; my mother yelled at the top of her lungs; "What?!" Then, I recall Adrienne sticking a knife in the sides of the trunk trying to get an opening and at the same time, my mother trying to get the key to work. I believe that I was about 7 years old. It was getting hard to breathe inside. It was hot and I was sweating. I was cramped up and uncomfortable. Suddenly, I remembered a conversation that I heard between our realtor, my mother and stepfather. It was about having to wait for an ambulance to come from Salisbury, MD to Ocean Pines, MD in case of an emergency. Salisbury was 22 minutes away. My mother had not even called the ambulance yet. I remember the thought coming into my head that I would be dead in 22 minutes. The idea just popped into my head to get on my hands and knees and pushed my back up like a cat with all my might until I busted the top of the chest and squeezed my little body out of the side. I still remember the shock on both Adrienne's and my mother's faces to see me busting through the chest. I now realize that it was God who told me when and what to do to save my life.

Cracks in the Potter's Clay

My mother raised my sister and I with freedom to explore and express ourselves. My mother's sister, Ruth, told me that my mother was reading a book on child rearing and read that it was not good to spank your children. I believe this was a mistake. My sister was very disrespectful to my mother. I believe if my mother would have spanked her more, she would not have been so disrespectful. I received one spanking from my mother and that was when I was around 6. Here is the reason why: My mother was on the porch talking to a woman and Adrienne and I were behind the front door making a lot of noise. Adrienne would tap on the glass to make them look at us and then stoop down out of site. I was just laughing and peeking out the window.

This went on for their entire conversation. I know it was embarrassing for my mother. Well, the woman left, and my mother turned around and looked at us looking out the front door with an expression of anger that scared me. As she reached for the door, I heard her say that she was going to spank us. I knew by the look in her eyes, that she meant it. I saw Adrienne get spanked before and I didn't want any parts of it so I ran and hid in my favourite hiding spot. It was a wooden dresser in the closet in my room that was missing the bottom drawer. I was so tiny, that I could fit my entire body inside of it. I heard Adrienne getting spanked and crying. Then there was silence. I heard my mother call me, but I did not answer. I heard Adrienne telling my mother that she knows where I always would hide.

I heard my mother outside of the closet. She called my name; "Allison, are you in there?" I remember answering; "Yes." She told me to come out. I asked her if I was going to get a spanking and she told me no. She lied! I came out and she sat on my bed and pulled me across her lap and spanked me. While the spanking hurt, I remembered crying and thinking: "She lied to me." That hurt me more. I had such a loving relationship with her, and she always told me that I was her joy. You do not spank your joy. Lol I do realize now that I should have come out when she called me. I only obeyed her because she said she would not spank me. That was the only time that she ever hit me. I continued to grow up hearing my sister disrespect my mother and my mother not disciplining her consistently. I know there were times that I needed discipline also.

My mother and father divorced when I was young. I believe I was 3 or4 years old. Adrienne, however, was two years older than me. She remembered my father better than I and had memories of him. She felt his absence. I only have one memory of my father and my mother in the house and that is an embarrassing memory. I had watched something on TV about stunt people. I was fascinated by Evil Kenevil. I saw someone control their body while falling down a flight of stairs. I remember practicing falling down the stairs slowly. Well, I remember calling my mother and father to come to the bottom of the stairs to watch me. I was at the top of the stairs. I said: "Watch this.' I proceeded my slow controlled descent, and something went wrong immediately. I tumbled all the way down the steps full speed landing at my parents' feet. How proud they must have been. Lol

The only other memory I have of my father, Ahmed (then Arnold), in the house was in the hallway by the front door. I was thirteen and I remember meeting my sister Amina (then her name was April) and my new stepmother Khadijah (then her name was Kathy). My father, stepmother and sister were standing together. I remember how cute my little sister was. She was so shy and had the sweetest smile I had ever seen. My father had moved to Minneapolis shortly after my parents divorced and I only saw him a few times growing up.

My mom remarried Joseph Coursey when I was maybe 5 or 6 and they separated a couple times during their marriage, the last time when I was 13. They remained separated and married until his death during my first semester of college. I remember him being very encouraging to me and very mean whenever he drank too much. He was an alcoholic. When Pop, as we called him, was sober, he was a man of integrity. He would always say that nothing was too good for his "tomatoes." Adrienne and I were his tomatoes. He referred to Mommy as Prime Rib. After they separated, I would catch a Greyhound bus to Atlantic City to visit him. Once, I asked him why he did not find someone else and this is what he told me: "Allison, once you have had Prime Rib, you don't want ground beef anymore." He was a cook but would not allow me in the kitchen while he was cooking. The years that he was with us were made up of good times, laughter, yelling and cursing.

I was afraid of him when he was drunk, so I did everything he told me to do without hesitation. Adrienne resented him from the very beginning. I think because she remembered our father and did not like a man that was not her father telling her what to do. She would resist his efforts to discipline. An example of Pop's alcoholic abusive behavior was one night during our first summers in

Cracks in the Potter's Clay

Ocean Pines.   Adrienne was talking back to him. He became furious and grabbed her around her throat.   Well, my mother did not play that.   She punched Pop across the face causing his black eyeglasses to go sailing across the room.   He was legally blind.   I remember him yelling: "You have done it now Joan!   You never knock a blind man's glasses off his face!"

He stormed back into the bedroom and got his gun. (He kept his loaded gun on the nightstand and told Adrienne and I never to touch it.   We never did.   My mother said she was so relieved when someone broke into our house and stole that gun.)   He stopped in the kitchen and got a large two prong carving fork and set the gun on the end table next to my mother.   She was seated in a chair.   I was kneeling on the floor next to her crying and looking out the sliding glass door into the darkness. Adrienne was next to me. It was pitch black outside except for the lights of Ocean City across the bay.

He then went and sat across the room at the dining room table grasping the fork in his hand.   He told my mother to pick up the gun and try to shoot him and threatened her that if she did try, he would run across the room and pierce her heart with the fork before she could even pick up the gun.   Being so young, and imagining my sweet mother being stabbed with a fork made me start crying harder and I started begging her not to try it. She calmly said: "It's ok baby. Mommy is not going to do that." Then all our attention was drawn to headlights of a car moving very slowly in front of our house. It was a police car. Evidently someone heard the yelling and crying and called the police.

Pop was only in Ocean Pines during the summer on the weekends. My mother would drive to Ocean City Friday evenings and pick him up at the Trailways bus station. He would work all week and join us on the weekends. We would drop him off on Sunday evenings to return to Baltimore. I loved that my mother was a teacher because I had her on the weekends, holidays and summers. During the school year, my mother began to remove herself and my sister and I from Pop's alcoholic abusive behavior by taking us to the Arena Playhouse with her. The Arena Playhouse is an historic African American Theatre in Baltimore, MD. The early rehearsals for plays were not in the existing theatre but at the Community College of Baltimore aka CCB. It is now Baltimore City Community College aka BCCC. Rehearsals were also held at a three-story row home on McCullough Street. I recall a rather scary event that also happened when I was 7.

Cracks in the Potter's Clay

My mother and the other actors tended to stand outside the building after rehearsals and talk to each other. McCullough Street was not in the best of neighbourhoods as we were about to find out. My sister remembers this story so well. She saw a man walking up the street and she remembered feeling afraid. She
said she told our mother to hurry up and to get in the car. My mother did not listen. Unfortunately, when the man Adrienne saw walking towards us reached us, he grabbed Adrienne (9 yrs old) around the throat and said: "I have a gun in this bag and I will kill this young b&^ch if y'all don't give me all of your money!"

My mother simultaneously yelled "Get your hands off my daughter!" while delivering a Bruce Lee chop to the man's arm, knocking the bag with the gun in it he was holding to the ground. My mother's actions took the man off guard and he took off running. Tony Carpenter, who was playing the role of Jesus in a play at the time, took off running after him. I remember being so afraid that I just started crying. My mother was so shaken up that she could not open the car door. She kept turning the key back and forth locking and unlocking the door. Tony ended up catching the man and he was arrested. Adrienne had to go to court to identify him. She was very traumatized.

She still remembers his name. So do I. I recall the next rehearsals being at the theater.

From age 7 to around age 15, my mother either acted in or directed every play of every season at the Playhouse. My sister and I brought the term 'Theater brats' to life. We knew every inch of that theater. Adrienne was always the ringleader and would have me upstairs in the attic trying on costumes or running around the building top speed while our mother was rehearsing. Sometimes child actors were needed. Mommy would make us play the roles. When I was not exploring with Adrienne, I was watching my mother act. She was exceptionally talented. I especially enjoyed watching her act in musicals. I loved how she moved. She had such rhythm and could make a simple movement look grand. My mentor, Les Brown, always says that some things are taught, and some things are caught. I caught a lot watching my mother perform.

Being so heavily involved in the theater was great for my memory. I remember cueing my mother which was holding the playbook and reading the other character's roles while Mommy said her lines. I would tell her if she got any words wrong or if she missed any words. No wonder I found it easy to learn Spanish. I already knew how to memorize. The Arena Playhouse put on a wonderful variety of comedies, musicals and dramas. We knew all the regular actors there. We even went to all the cast parties. They were held after the last performance of a show. Everyone knew Joan's daughters. If you saw Joan, you saw her daughters. I was always so proud to be her daughter. In every play I saw my mother act in, no matter how big or small the part, she always got a standing ovation.

My mother got a double Master's degree in Speech and Theater from New York University. Two of her classmates were Esther Rolle (Florida on TV show Good Times) and Louis Gossett Jr. (Fiddler from movie Roots). She got both to come to the Arena Playhouse once. I remember Louis Gossett Jr. being genuinely nice. He was my mother's first boyfriend at age 22. She was super driven and focused while in high school and college. She told me that all their white classmates pushed them so hard to be a couple that it ruined the relationship. My mother was stunning. (As you can see from the cover portrait) Louis Gossett Jr. was very handsome. My mother said her classmates insisted that they were perfect for each other, it did not seem natural, and the relationship did not prosper but they remained friends. They kept in touch after graduation and her move back to Baltimore.

My teenage years were characterized by lots of ups and downs. Bipolar 1 Disorder is characterized by extreme highs and extreme lows. The extreme highs are referred to as states of mania or manic episodes. The extreme lows are characterized by depression or hopelessness. During mania, a Bipolar I person is so physically active and awake for long periods of time and not aware that the body needs rest that eventually a crash occurs. The crash is caused from physical and mental exhaustion but the symptoms get attributed to depression. This is what I have learned about myself. Therefore, I don't make important decisions when I am exhausted and I have learned not to even trust my feelings during this time because they are usually inaccurate. When you are not well rested, your thoughts are not the same thoughts you have when you are rested.

When I was a teenager, I remember my mother saying: "Allison you are either up or you are down. There is not an in-between with you." She did not even realize that she was diagnosing me. But I was just her daughter whom she loved. She did not take me to be evaluated. She accepted me for who I was and showed me unconditional love. I remember her making the statement, but I don't remember her attaching any emotion to it, be it negative or positive. I never thought twice about it until I was diagnosed with Bipolar 1 at age 33 and was told about the symptoms.

Pop and my mother separated when I was around 13 years old. My mother was saved by then and had asked God for a sign to stay together with him or not. RIght after she prayed, he got drunk and embarrassed her at the Arena Playhouse by yelling and cursing. She asked him to leave the house and he left. She had purchased the house before they were married. I took it hard because I really loved him. He soon moved back to Atlantic City, New Jersey.

I really missed him. He had been so encouraging to me. I became depressed. I began smoking cigarettes out of rebellion and stopped going to church with my mother so often. I would only go on Sundays. I began searching for love in older men who were more than willing to take advantage of a young, pretty girl with an athletic body. I mistakenly thought that if I slept with a man, he would love me and marry me. Not only was that not true but my first three boyfriends, all considerably older than me, married the next woman after me. It was devastating for me. I remember thinking: "What is wrong with me? Why don't men love me? I gave them my body."

Another incident that reminds me of God's presence in my life is when I was a freshman at Hampton University. I bought a motorcycle because freshmen could not have cars on campus there. I had gotten my driver's license as soon as I turned sixteen and I was not about to go back to walking when I had been so accustomed to driving. I was spoiled at that time. One day I was polishing my motorcycle on the side of Davidson Hall, which was the dormitory that I stayed in during my year at Hampton University. I felt homesick. I think that this was the first Bipolar 1 impulse that I gave into. Hampton was 4 hours away from Baltimore. I simply climbed on my bike and headed for Baltimore.

I took route 17 because it was very scenic. Unfortunately, it was very hilly also. My motorcycle was a small bike. It was a Honda C125S. It only went up to 80 mph and it used to stall when trying to make it up steep hills. It would just cut off and I would have to get to the side of the road to kick start it again and maybe replace a fuse. I was driving and I noticed that I would soon be approaching a series of big hills. To make it over a hill, I used to drive fast so that I could coast forward if the bike stalled. I made it over the first hill. I made it over the second hill. The third hill was the steepest.

I remember having a feeling of doom. Nonetheless, I maxed the mph to 80. I made it to about 200 feet from the top of the hill and my bike engine cut off. I was in the fast lane. My heart dropped in fear that the bike would decelerate quickly, and I would get run over by a car behind me. Well, it turned out that when I looked in the rear-view mirror, there were no cars behind me or beside me. I immediately thanked God and was able to coast over from the fast lane to the right shoulder. I began to walk and push the bike up the hill and like a miracle, at the top of the hill was a gas station.

I gassed up, which only took $1.75 to fill up the tank, replaced the fuse and got back on the road. It was early wintertime and I had only worn a jean jacket. The later it got in the evening, the lower the temperature dropped. I remember being at two hours from Baltimore when I first began to shiver. When I reached home, I went straight to my Aunt Ruth's house. She was my mother's only sister. I figured my mother would still be at church. She was saved by then and was wearing many hats at the church like Pastor's Aide, Head of the TV, Radio and Drama Ministries. She was also working on her third master's degree. This one in Divinity from St. Mary's Seminary, Baltimore, MD.

I went inside my aunt's house and I remember it took me a long time to stop shivering. Aunt Ruth had gone to Bingo. I was sitting on the couch in the living room waiting for her. When my aunt arrived home, she came through the front door announcing: "Somebody's got a motorcycle outside that looks just like Allison's!" Then she saw me and screamed: "Oh my Lord!" No one could believe that I had driven that motorcycle four hours by myself. I was 18 years old. I did not understand why everyone thought that was so amazing. I just wanted to go home. I had transportation and I never felt alone. I recall my mother bragging to others of my response when she asked me if I was afraid being alone on the road. My response was "I wasn't alone. God was with me." My mother developed great faith and was happy my faith was developing.

James 4:8 Draw near to God and He will draw near to you. I believe that I was 17 when I walked the aisle to accept Jesus as my Savior at Bethel AME Church in Baltimore, Maryland where my mother was the Assistant Pastor. The Pastor at that time was Rev. John R. Bryant (now Bishop John R.

Bryant). I remember that night when I drank the tiny communion cup. I felt a sensation like water rushing down my throat and into my lungs. I told my mother about it and she told me that it was the Holy Spirit. I started to learn more about God by attending church regularly with my mother. I really enjoyed the singing of the Jones Brothers and the Imani Messengers Choir and all the hymns that they used to sing.

Pop died during my first semester at Hampton University. I was majoring in Architecture instead of Art because Pop wanted me to. I got really depressed after he died. I stayed to myself and focused heavily on my architecture projects. One day I was walking across campus to my dormitory when I saw a man playfully chasing a small boy around the yard. I don't know what it was about this man but I stopped walking and just watched him from afar. My heart was fluttering. I then saw my dorm director, Pat White and thought that the man was her boyfriend or husband. I snapped out of the daze I was in and continued to my dorm room thinking no more of this man.

One day a friend of mine named Nicole came to Bemus, the architecture building to find me. She said that she had someone she wanted me to meet. I told her that I was not interested in dating anyone. She said: "You don't have to marry the man. I just want you to meet him." She convinced me that I had been depressed long enough about my stepfather and that I should get away from schoolwork for a while. I agreed to go with her. She was dating this guy's friend named Jeff. Jeff was driving a black, two door Ford EXP. Nichole was sitting in the passenger seat of the two-seater. I crawled in the back of the car and looked out the big rear window. We went to Langley Air Force Base to some barracks. Nicole and Jeff walked in front of me and when we reached the guy's room, Jeff told me to knock on the door because he was expecting me.

I knocked lightly on the door I heard a voice say: "Come in." When I saw this man sitting on the bed, I had the same feeling I felt when I was walking across campus and saw that man. It felt so strong that I had to look away. When I looked away, I saw a vision of my mother and father with their wedding attire on. I thought to myself: "Is this going to be my husband?" I told myself to be cool. We both fell in love hard and fast. We talked all night and when I got back to my dorm room, I received a knock on the door that I had a phone call. I never got phone calls. My mother would write me letters and send me money but I did not get calls. I was so happy to find out that this tall, dark, handsome man had called me and wanted to talk to me for two more hours.

Douglas Landell Hall and I were married a little more than three months later. We had two children during our union, Joshua Landell Hall and Christina Joan Hall. They are twenty months apart. My sister and I were twenty-three months apart. I had Christina so Joshua would have someone to play with growing up. Douglas was an excellent provider. I tried to be an excellent housewife and loved to take care of him. I got pregnant right after we got married. My neighbor Mrs. Smith was a housewife and I admired her being home with her children. I was thankful to be a housewife. I had breakfast on the table for Douglas before he left for work, lunch on the table when he arrived home for lunch and dinner on the table when he got home from dinner. I kept the house neat and ironed his uniforms. I do remember being tired while I was pregnant and sleeping a lot. I remember waking up a couple hours before he came home just to clean the house and cook before he got home. Lol

I had completed one full year at Hampton University before we got married. I loved Douglas because he was the first man that loved me enough to marry me and then he was willing to give me children. The happiest day of my life was when I married Douglas. I remember sitting on the steps in the back of the Bethel AME Church in my wedding gown with a huge smile on my face. The sun was shining through the church doors and I was simply elated. My father even flew from Minneapolis to give me away. As he was walking me down the aisle, I whispered to him "Daddy, I am scared." His response was "Me too." Lol

Douglas left me in Baltimore with my mom for a few weeks after we were married and rented us a townhouse at West County Townhouses right around the corner from Hampton University. He then came back to Baltimore to take me to our new home. We loaded my bedroom furniture up in the U-Haul and left for Hampton. Correction, Douglas, Adrienne and my mother loaded the U-Haul. I had my regular horrific monthly cramps and I couldn't help. I would miss a day from school every month because I would vomit, have diarrhea and have horrible cramps the first day of my period. The doctors told me that they would most likely stop after I had my first child. They did. I can still see my mother and sister in the doorway holding each other crying as we pulled off. I was crying too. I was moving out of state. The three of us were close.

Cracks in the Potter's Clay

When I was eight months pregnant with Joshua, I met my best friend, Jean.   Douglas and her then husband, Paul had been stationed together in Florida. Paul stopped over with Jean and their sons Byron and Josiah. Josiah was only six months old. I shared our dinner with them. I believe that there is always enough to share. Well, Jean invited us to dinner the next week. Did I mention that Jean is Filipino? Jeannie is the best cook ever. I absolutely loved her Pancit, Lumpia and Adobo. I had never tasted food so good. I was so excited the following week when she invited us to dinner again. I was pregnant, fat and hungry all the time. I recall reaching her front door but did not smell any food cooking like I did the last time I was there.

I walked in and saw several ladies sitting on the couch with gifts in front of them. Then I saw a cake and chips. Jeannie then said: "Ally, this is for you. These are women from my church. We are giving you a baby shower." This act touched my heart tremendously. How did she get people that did not even know me to buy me and my baby gifts? I would not have had a baby shower if it were not for her. I loved Jeannie from that day on. I confessed years later that I was still disappointed that she did not cook. Lol She is one of the kindest and giving people that I know. I learned so much

from Jeannie, her being a little older and already having two children. We
lived on base housing together. She would come upstairs everyday with the Pan de Sal and I would make us coffee and we would do my exercise video Callanetics.

The second happiest day of my life was when I gave birth to Joshua and the third happiest day was when I gave birth to Christina. However, Christina's delivery was difficult. I was in labor for 12 hours with my son, Joshua and vowed to never that again. Then I thought Joshua would be lonely growing up without a playmate and I had forgotten about the pain, so we got pregnant with Christina. I knew the moment that I conceived her. Joshua was five months old when Douglas came home on leave from Korea. He had sent home some wooden wind chimes to me and I had hung them above the bed. (I did not know what they were when I was 20.) Well, when we were doing the horizontal mambo, the wind chimes began to move as if a huge wind blew. Douglas stopped for a minute because it was startling. I looked at the window and it was not even open. I knew that I was pregnant.

Cracks in the Potter's Clay

I only waited two weeks to go to Wyman Park Hospital to get a pregnancy test. They said that you had to wait four weeks after a skipped period for the test to be accurate. I lied and said it had been four weeks. It came back positive. I was overjoyed. I was in labor for 22 and a half hours with Christina and she kept turning sideways inside of me. I had to breathe through contractions while the doctor put his hands in order to turn her around. He removed his hands and she turned back around. The second time he did it, I felt life slipping away from me and I yelled for my savior at the top of my lungs: "Jeeeeeeeesssuuuuuuus!!!" A peace came over me immediately. The doctor said that it was finally time to go into the delivery room.

Time To Go To Work

Christina was three months when funds became a little tight. Douglas and I decided that I would start working part-time after he got home from work. I started working part time as a waitress at a Thai restaurant. I was still nursing her. Douglas wanted me to quit that job after the first day because Christina didn't want to drink the breast milk from the bottle. My mother named me Allison. It spells All is on. That had always been my motto. If there was a way to do something that I wanted to do, I would always find that way. I did not want to quit after only one day, so I explained the problem to the manager. I was such a good worker that she told me that I could bring Christina to work with me and put her in the far corner of the kitchen in a swing. I would take her into the bathroom to nurse her. No wonder she grew up loving to cook. The cooks adored her. One of them used to call her Meatball because her cheeks were so fat that it looked like she had meatballs in her cheeks. They worked me too hard there. I was not only the only waitress, but I had to bus my own tables and set up my own tables after that. I soon got a job as a waitress at the NCO Club. By this time, Christina started to take the bottle for her father.

Soon, I realized that my working part-time as a waitress and Douglas' income would not be enough to award my children the same lifestyle that I had growing up. I always heard people say that they wanted better for their children than what they had. I decided to go back to school so I could get a job that paid more. I had gone to private, Catholic schools and we had a summer home. I could not provide that for my children on a part-time waitress salary.

Thankfully, I left Hampton University in good standing and went to see about re-enrolling. It was too expensive. My mother offered to pay but I told her that I was married now and that I was not her responsibility any longer. All is on. I applied for and received a Pell Grant and first attended Thomas Nelson Community College with a major in Fine Arts. There was enough money left over from tuition and buying books that I was able to buy Douglas a white guitar for his birthday. I was so excited. He absolutely loves the artist Prince and is a very gifted musician. He taught himself to play many instruments.

I recall laying in the bed while I was pregnant with Joshua listening to him create music. I was his number one fan. When he would finish the song that he was working on, I would yell to him: "Go head Doug!!! That sounded so good!!" My mother instilled the importance of education in me at an early age and it was never an option to not go to college. I always worked hard to get good grades. College was no different. I am an "A" student. I do what I must do to get what I want. I put in the study time. My gift was Art but I developed a passion for the Spanish language. Thomas Nelson had a professor named Gloria Smith who I simply adored. She used to write comments on all my papers and tell me what a good student I was. I have always responded well to encouragement. I worked even harder for her. Then I took advantage of the opportunity to have a Spanish tutor. It was free for students. I wanted to practice conversational Spanish. My tutor's name was Marco Camion and he was from Lima, Peru.

I would meet with Marco in the cafeteria and would even call him on the phone to practice speaking. I still remember how his mother answered the phone: "Alo?" She had the sweetest voice and loved to talk to me. Our free sessions came to an end one day when Mrs. Smith came to me and asked what I was doing. She told me that I was making straight "A's" and that she needed me as a tutor. I did not realize I was that good. I began tutoring and getting paid for it and students' grades went up. After graduating with honors from Thomas Nelson, I transferred to Christopher Newport University where I received a partial minority academic scholarship. I majored in Fine Art again but had extra scholarship money, so I took extra courses in Spanish because I loved it so.

I was happy in my marriage with Douglas for 8 years. We had our ups and downs, but we were basically happy. We loved our children and were responsible parents. We lived on Langley Air Force Base. It reminded me of Ocean Pines because it was right on the waterfront. I would take the kids to visit my family in Baltimore when I could and my mother and sister, Adrienne would come and visit us often. Adrienne didn't have any children, but she loved being Aunt Adrienne. She loved to shower the kids with gifts. One of the best memories that I have of my mother was at Latin Night at the NCO Club.

Every Friday, they would have a Latin Night in the ballroom. They had a live salsa band. I would finish waitressing and sneak through the kitchen door and dance and practice my Spanish. I was never taught how to Salsa, but I could follow well. My mother used to be a dancer with the Catherin Dunham dance group right out of high school. She travelled throughout Europe with the group. She was, at the time, an ordained minister. This night, I convinced my mother to join me for Latin Night. I know that I got my gift of dance from her and I knew that she would love it. Well, she went.

The ballroom was packed with people. The orchestra was in rare form. My mother and I were both asked to dance right away. The dance floor stayed full all night. I did not see my mother again until they brought the lights up at 3:00 am. Me and my dance partner and my mother and her dance partner were the only four people left on the floor! Best memory ever! She was so happy and so was I. She was imitating the men asking her: "Where you learn to salsa like dat girl?" We were African American women of non-Hispanic origin, but we could dance the Salsa and Merengue so well.

The End of My First Marriage

First, Jean's husband, Paul got stationed in Saudi Arabia during the Desert Storm war and then Douglas got stationed there. I helped Jean during her meltdown when Paul was away, and she helped me during mine when Douglas was away. A combination of things changed in our marriage when Douglas got back from Saudi. He seemed different. I was different also. I was still in college and I had become more independent. He was not my whole world anymore. There was something else that affected our relationship. It was a case of mistaken identity. One of Douglas' friends told him that they saw me going into a hotel room with this club manager who was Hispanic. Douglas had seen us speaking Spanish together before. It was not me though. It was someone who looked like me. I do know the person and I know that they went to the hotel together because the person told me.

Unfortunately, he did not ask me about this. I admit that I was behaving differently and wanted more freedom. I even lied to him that I was over a girlfriend's house when I was over a male friend's house. I got busted because he had called my friend's house and I was not there. Nothing sexual was going on. The classmate was just nice to me and it seemed like Douglas did not like me anymore. I just wanted to be happy and feel good about myself for a while. I think because of that lie, he chose to believe what he heard about me. He began to treat me mean and even called me out of my name. He had never called me out of my name.

I did not understand why he was being so mean to me. Once, while we were arguing, I looked at my children and they were sitting on the floor crying and holding each other. It reminded me of me crying while my mother and stepfather were arguing. I decided then that I was not going to subject my children to that. I ended up leaving with the children to live in a shelter. I just wanted peace. After living in the shelter for a year, I went back to him and that is when he told me that his friend saw me at the hotel. I told him it was not me and I think he believed me, but he still seemed upset with me. The arguing began again, and I left again with the kids. The shelters in Hampton were not bad at all. They were clean and because I followed the rules, the kids and I ended up with our own apartment.

After Douglas and I separated in April of 1993 and I graduated from college in May of 1994, my mother asked me to come back home to Baltimore. I became a high school Spanish and Art teacher. Our children grew up in Baltimore and attended private Catholic schools through 9th grade like I had done growing up. I only attended private Catholic schools until the 7th grade because of the financial hardship my mother was going through due to her separation from my stepfather. I was feeling like I was giving my children more than I had. I took them to church regularly. My mother was a great inspiration to me spiritually and I tried to emulate her love for the Lord and others. I was affectionate giving my children plenty of hugs and smiles growing up like my mother gave me.

Chapter 2: The Cracks

April 4, 1995, 11:59 pm. Adrienne was lucky to have this balcony outside of her bedroom. It was so quiet that night. The sky was very dark, making the moon hiding behind the tree branches look extra white. As usual, it felt like I was the only one awake in the world. A song from one of the plays Mommy directed at the Arena Players came to my mind and I started singing it: "Moon outside my window, shining down on me. I don't want you to see how lonely I can be." I lit up another cigarette using the embers from the one that I had just finished. "Forgive me for smoking Lord. Please don't let me get lung cancer." I remembered looking at my watch and thinking to myself: "God is going to take her home on my birthday." I finished smoking and got in the bed and went to sleep.

1 Samuel 3:7-8 Now Samuel did not yet know the LORD, neither was the word of the LORD yet revealed unto him. And the LORD called Samuel again the third time. And he arose and went to Eli, and said, here am I; for thou didst call me. And Eli perceived that the LORD had called the child.

I was awakened by the phone at 4:10 am. It was Dr. Aisner. "I'm sorry to tell you that your mother passed away at 4:05 this morning." It was my 29th birthday. I called Douglas but could not form the words to say it. I was crying. He said: "I'm on my way." I felt that he loved me on that day. I was priority this time, not the Air Force. He drove from Hampton, Virginia in record time. It was usually a 4-hour trip and he arrived in a little more than 3 hours. He loved and respected my mother also. We were separated but we still cared about each other enough to have a good relationship for the children's sake.

We both love our children. I am so glad that I came home when my mother invited me back home. Those are 10 months that I got to spend with my mother that I would not have had if I had not moved back home. She so enjoyed spending time with her grandchildren Joshua 8 and Christina 6. We attended several of her one woman shows through Young Audiences of Maryland. She taught and sang about African American history as a griot.

34

Cracks in the Potter's Clay

She even incorporated some of the songs that she used to sing to my sister and I while growing up. Children loved my mother's performances and so did I. I never grew tired of watching my mother perform. She passed 25 years ago.

Now that I know God's voice, I know that it was Him trying to prepare me by telling me in advance that my beautiful, kind, loving, brilliant and talented mother, Reverend Dr. Joan Rebecca Coursey, age 59, was going to die on my birthday; April 5, 1995. They say that the onset of Bipolar could be the result of a traumatic event. I used to think I became Bipolar after my mother died on my birthday. I really could not grieve. I had two young children that I was raising alone, and I had to be strong for them. My sister on the other hand would call me while she was sprawled out on her kitchen floor screaming to the top of her lungs. I cried at times but most of the time, I pushed it down for my children's sake so that I could focus on them.

For several years after she passed, I would have manic episodes in the months preceding both her birthday and my birthday. The first three years I made big plans for my birthday so that I would not focus on the great loss. The first year, I went on a Sun Princess cruise where my uncle Terry Johnson of the original Flamingos was performing with my aunt Theresa. The second year, I was in a relationship with a famous actor. Ben Vereen from the movie Roots by Alex Haley. Funny how my mother and I both dated men that were in that movie. She dated Fidler and I dated Chicken George. Lol The third year, I got married to a man that I barely knew that turned out to be abusive. That marriage only lasted one month. The fourth year I got in a serious relationship with my now third ex-husband, Andre. In hindsight, I can see how my subconscious mind was at work. I married my second husband in a black mini-skirt suit on the anniversary of the date that we buried my mother, which was April 10th. I noticed it when I came across my mother's obituary some months later.

It was the first year after my mother passed that I first heard His voice. It was March and I had put an $800.00 deposit down to go study Spanish abroad in Mexico. It was a dream of mine to study abroad ever since I was in college on work study and a professor was bragging about one of her students winning a Fulbright Hayes Scholarship to study abroad. It sounded so exciting. I was a first-year provisional Spanish teacher and had never been to a Hispanic country. The French teachers that I worked with had gone to France and the Spanish teachers had gone to Spain or other Hispanic countries. I felt I was not as good as they were because I had never studied abroad.

This night, I was studying for a Spanish culture class exam. It was around 12 midnight. Joshua and Christina were asleep, and I was reading a story in Spanish when I heard a voice say: "Don't leave your kids." It startled me because I was reading in Spanish and I heard the voice in English. It seemed too strange for me to deal with, so I ignored it and went back to reading in Spanish. I then heard it again but louder. "Don't leave your kids!" Ok. Time for a cigarette. That is how I dealt with stress back then. I went out on the back porch and lit up a Newport 100 and began to think about what had just happened. I said to myself: "Don't leave your kids? Why not?

Suddenly, different scenarios began to run through my mind. What if something happened to one of them while I was in Mexico? I would not be able to be there to comfort them right away. What if something happened to me while I was in Mexico. Their father was living four hours away in Hampton, VA. I was planning to leave them for eight weeks in the summer with my cousin Edythe who does not drive. (However, she was a master at public transportation, and I know she would have taken great care of them.) Up to that point in their lives, I was always the one who take them to the doctors, cared for them when they were sick and who drove them everywhere. I took them everywhere with me like my mother took my sister and I everywhere with her.

Joshua and Christina never had a babysitter or went to childcare. Like me, they only visited my two Aunt Ruths. My mother's sister Ruth (She had a mole on her nose) and my mother's aunt Ruth (She did not have a mole on her nose). Whenever one of them would call the house, we would say: It's Aunt Ruth with the mole on her nose." or "It's Aunt Ruth with no mole on her nose." My mother took me and my sister Adrienne everywhere with her and I gladly took my children everywhere with me. The only time my children and I were ever separated until they were adults was when they stayed with my cousin Edythe and great aunt Ruth, with no mole on her nose, during my last 4 weeks of college. Living in the shelter, working part-time, taking a full load in college and caring for the children alone had gotten to be too much for me.

Thanks to Cousin Edythe and Aunt Ruth with no mole on her nose taking care of my children those four weeks, I graduated from Christopher Newport University with departmental honours earning a Bachelor of Fine Arts in Studio Art with a 3.57 GPA in 1994. I graduated from college exactly ten years after I graduated from high school. It is never too late to finish your education. I did not major in Spanish, but I absolutely loved the language. Since I had extra scholarship money, I took extra courses in Spanish. I practiced my Spanish while I was working at the NCO club whenever I recognized a Hispanic accent.

What I loved, was that every Hispanic that I practiced with, encouraged me and told me that my Spanish was good. Encouragement has always been important in my life. After my mother's death in 1995, I had begun to take Joshua and Christina to visit their father in Hampton, VA and grandmother in Stony Creek, VA. Someone must have been watching our house because my house was broken into while we were away. We came back to find items stacked by the windows as if someone were passing items out the window to another person. When the police arrived, they said that it looked like whoever it had been, left in a hurry. They did not take anything. I believe my mother, or a guardian angel scared them away.

My cousin Charles said that he felt a presence in the house after my mother passed. A friend of Andre and I named Ivy said that he saw a woman in a white dress out of the corner of his eye while sitting in the den watching TV. He said it freaked him out. The fact that someone had broken into the house did alarm me. I decided to sign the three of us up for karate. I imagined we would be like the' Three Ninjas' and could together defeat anyone that broke into the house. It also gave us something positive to focus on while we were grieving. We attended Joe Palanzo's Kenpo Karate school and that is where I met my third husband, Andre. He was an amazing martial artist and teacher to me and the kids. He was so very encouraging.

Once we started competing, he would coach me and lead me to victory. He would tell me: "Allison, you can beat her. Axe-kick her on the head." I have high kicks because of my dance background. I did what he told me to do and won all my matches. We all had a ball traveling and competing in tournaments. Andre really loves Joshua and Christina, and they love him too. They scared me so badly one day. The karate studio was in a shopping centre with many stores. After practice, I went to change out of my Gi and when I came out of the dressing room Joshua and Christina were nowhere to be found. I panicked. I always knew where my children were.

Cracks in the Potter's Clay

I looked throughout the school and had just taken off running down the steps to the outside when these three jokers came walking through the school door smiling and laughing. I was furious because he took my children to the store to buy them something without asking me first. I yelled at all three of them, grabbed Joshua and Christina by the arms and left. I eventually cooled off and we returned to karate.

We continued to study Kenpo and began moving up in belts. Andre and some of his karate friends branched out on their own to open their own karate studio called Five Point Kenpo Karate. We followed them to three different locations. Andre and I and the kids enjoyed each other's company so much that we decided to get married in June of 1999. Andre was doing everything to impress me while we were dating. He used to come to my hairdressers every week and pay to get my hair done and would take us out to eat a lot. He was spoiling me. I recall telling him that if he was not going to keep this up after we got married to please stop then. I told him that I would not take it well if he changed after we got married. He said things would get even better.

Unfortunately, as soon as we got married, his behaviour changed. I reminded him of our conversation when I told him that I would divorce him if he changed negatively. I was very frustrated, and my behaviour demonstrated my displeasure. I would cuss and I would fuss but to no avail. At one time, I thought about leaving because Andre and the kids were getting along wonderfully. I was the only one unhappy. I did not leave because we were living in the house that my mother left my sister and I. I bought my sister out with inheritance money our mother left us. You see, living in a shelter for a year gave me the desire to have my own home.

Being a Christian, I often reflected on my behaviour. I would feel ashamed and would go to Andre and apologize. I was feeling out of control. I was extremely disappointed at how things changed after we got married. The spoiling stopped. I tried to force him to treat me the way I wanted him to. I yelled, I cursed, and I withheld sex. Nothing worked. It only made me feel bad about myself. One Sunday while at Christian Life Church, I heard a sermon about being marred in the potters' hands. It touched my heart. I went to the altar for prayer. While at the altar, I heard a voice say: "Something is wrong with you."

The next day I went to Andre's primary care doctor, Doctor Siegel. I disclosed my feelings about Andre to him and he said that he thought that I was Bipolar. I was not expecting that response. I was talking about Andre. How did it get turned around on me? Nonetheless, All is on. That is my name. I went to him for help. I wanted to improve the quality of my life. I was optimistic and relentless in seeking happiness. Doctor Siegel referred me to a psychiatrist, and I began taking medicine at the end of 1999.

The medicine, or shall I say, my belief in the medicine, appeared to be helping after a few weeks. Over the months and years when the stress of marriage became too difficult, I would go to the doctor and have him change or increase my medicine. The medicines that I took over the years were: Depakote, Celexa, Wellbutrin, Vrylar, Lamictil, Lithium, Trazodone and Topamax for migraines. I also took Pravastatin for borderline cholesterol for many years. I took psychotropic drugs for 20 years. I have been free from all drugs including the Pravastatin for over a year. It is January 31, 2021, that I am writing this.

I am presently awaiting my daughter's feedback of growing up with a mother who was Bipolar. My son's greatest complaint is that I did not allow him to express himself. He said that it was my way or the highway. He also regrets the times that I spanked him with a belt across the behind. I have explained to him that I intentionally spanked them occasionally for bad behaviour while growing up because I was not disciplined enough as a child and it was miserable being spoiled. When things do not go your way, you behave badly. The Bible also says in Proverbs 13:24 Whoever spares the rod hates their children, but the one who loves their children is careful to discipline them. (New International Version.) He also just shared with me a few minutes ago that through his upbringing, he inherited the victim mindset. Wow. That was deep and so true.

There were other personal things that my son expressed to me during this conversation that were difficult to hear but I walk in truth now. I do not run from anything. I owned and acknowledged everything he said. He did not know it, but I was crying as he was saying his goodbye and thanking me for listening. He is a gracious and great orator. Joshua expresses himself eloquently. He has written hundreds of rap songs and made a CD with his cousin Steve in 2009. I was his number one fan. He is incredibly talented. I feel he will write a book one day and it is going to be a bestseller. I am praying for strength that when my daughter gets back to me with feedback, it will be just as productive.

Cracks in the Potter's Clay

Since I am in a self-reflective mindset, I decided to call my ex-husband, Andre and see if he wanted to share anything helpful about living with a wife with Bipolar 1. He was busy but the one sentence he did share was impactful to me. I asked him if he ever really understood my symptoms and could he distinguish them from my regular personality. He said: "I knew when it was full blown because you were either not doing anything or doing too much." We never used to discuss my symptoms. This is my first time feeling that he understood. That was such a profound statement about me. I would be so depressed at times, that I would just sleep or lay in the bed and not eat. Other times, I was cleaning the house from top to bottom and able to out-eat everyone, including him.

I know the cleaning sprees had an adverse reaction on Joshua, Christina and Andre. I would start cleaning and could not stop. I would become tired and instead of just stopping, I would become angry that no one was helping me. I would sometimes make the kids stop whatever they were doing, including sleeping, and make them help me. I would also start verbally attacking Andre and try to get him to help too. I remember the three of them whispering to each other about me and I remember feeling that I should just leave. The three of them got along fine together.

Remember I stated that Bipolar 1 people have a lot of energy and require little sleep? Well, the mind keeps the body going but the body is still under stress and responds. For me, it would respond aggressively with yelling and more aggressive behaviour. I am sure that, although I did not spank my kids a lot, most of the times that I did, I was angry. Joshua reminded me today that I did not explain in detail why he was being punished. I sucked at explaining why in detail! Oh, how I wish I knew better. My mentor Les Brown often says; If people knew better, they would do better. I never wanted to hurt anyone. I wanted to love everyone. Now, I know better.

Suicidal Thoughts and Wanting to Die

I was voluntarily hospitalized for inpatient stays three times and one outpatient stay. I weaned myself off of all but one medicine during the outpatient two week stay. I recall when I first was admitted for abruptly stopping my mood stabilizer, I had suicidal thoughts. I was sitting on the first row in church, and I saw a huge knife in my hands pointed towards my stomach. I saw myself thrust it into my stomach. It scared me and upset me so badly that I got up and ran out of the church. My children followed me. I went to my Cousin Edythe's house for consolation. My children and Andre followed me there. I thought it best to go to the hospital.

Once in the hospital and checked into my room after they took away my shoestrings, belt and mirror from my purse, I found myself choking myself. I screamed for someone to help me. It turns out that the medicine that I was taking had suicidal thoughts as a side effect. The most recent times that I wanted to be dead was because of the lack of communication with my children and one of my sisters. Someone close to my children told them a lie about me. I know this because my son indicated to me that he thought what I did was messed up.

When I asked him what I did, he told me. It was a boldfaced lie. I had done the opposite of what was told to him. I spent an entire afternoon Googling ways to kill myself. I even called my insurance company to find out if my life insurance policy would pay if it was a suicide. I was suicidal but I was not inconsiderate. I did not want Andre to come home and find that I had hung myself or in the tub drowned. I read how most times when you take pills, they end up pumping your stomach and you wake up feeling horrible. I thought about having an accident but worried that I might just mess myself up and live. I had convinced myself that God would understand if I killed myself. I realize now that it was an attack from satan. God wants us to have life and to have it more abundantly.

Chapter 3: The Potter

I joined St. John AME Church in Baltimore, MD on August 30, 2015.   God sent me to this church where the Pastor was Rev. Dr. Peggy E. Wall. My mother and her were awfully close friends.   They both were ordained as Reverends under Bishop John R. Bryant at Bethel AME Church in Baltimore, MD. She loved my mother so much that she told my mother while she was on her deathbed that if she ever got her own church, she would name the dance ministry after her.   Well, she kept her word. The day that I joined the church, Pastor Wall had me stand up while she said kind words about my mother. It was such a proud moment for me. I have always felt proud to be the Joan Coursey's daughter. I joined the Rev. Joan Coursey Sign and Dance Ministry also.

My mother joined the Katherine Dunham Dance Company right after graduating from Douglas High School in 1954. She travelled to Europe and performed with the dance company. I did not know this until after my mother passed. My cousin Angela Gray who I am close with, went to school with my mother. My mother was not a braggart. One story my father likes to tell me about my mother was when he found out that she knew how to play the piano. My father was playing Misty on his trumpet and my mother walked in the den, sat down at the piano and accompanied him. I guess her motto was, I can show you better than I could tell you.

I only knew that my mother was a dancer, actress and a majorette in high school because I saw pictures of her in her high school yearbook. Her poses showed her grace. She was ridiculously photogenic. I used to love to watch her move while she was performing in plays whether they were musicals or drama. She made every step and wave of her arm memorable. She was pure grace in motion. My mentor Les Brown always says that some things are taught, and some things are caught. I did not realize how much I moved like my mother until after she passed, and I began my own dance ministry being led by the Holy Spirit.

Cracks in the Potter's Clay

November 4, 2018 marks the day God began His ministry through me. I became a Steward under Pastor Wall which is an appointed spiritual leader in the AME church. Every first Sunday, the Stewards would take turns delivering a meditation called Love Feast. November 4th was my turn and God had been speaking to me. I decided to just include the meditation just as I wrote it back in 2018. At the time I was estranged from all my immediate family and was staying with my cousin Judy who is my father's first cousin. We are awfully close. Here is the Love Feast:

"Life is not always easy. We all have a story to tell. We all suffer loss. We all have pain in our bodies at times. We all have been hurt by someone that we loved. We all have felt disappointment. We have all been confused at one time or another. We have all felt depressed. Life is not always easy. I would like to share some scriptures and thoughts that have helped make my life easier.

Joshua 1:8 Study this book of instruction continually. Meditate on it day and night so you will be sure to obey everything written in it. Only then will you prosper and succeed in all you do. That is a promise. The goal is to obey everything written in it. Because we are all sinners, it is impossible to be perfect and obey everything, but

God knows that. He honours His Word when we try. All we must do is try our best. I try my best and God lets me prosper and succeed in all I do. To me success is doing God's will. If I try to do something that is not in His will for me, and I fail, I do not see that as a failure. That is a success. The devil was defeated.

How I meditate on it day and night is: I read the New International Version Bible on my own every day and utilize a study Bible also. I also read scriptures that Doris Dobson, a church choir member and friend, sends me every day. I study the Word by reading commentaries in my Bible and look up different interpretations until I get an understanding. I listen to His Word preached by Pastor Wall and other preachers that I search on Youtube like Joyce Meyers, Creflo Dollar and Dale Bronner. I listen to hymns and Gospel music which have scriptures in them.

If I feel discouraged, for example, I will search for sermons on encouragement. If you search, God will make sure you find what you are looking for. It is His promise. Luke 11:9-10 "So I say to you: Ask and it will be given to you; seek and you will find; knock and the door will be opened to you. For everyone who asks receives; the one who seeks finds; and the one who knocks the door will be opened. If there is a scripture that I know, but I do not remember the address, He always lets me find it. In my searching, He also protects me from anything unlike Him. Sometimes, sermons on YouTube will not even open for me and I will just move on. His Word says, "And a stranger they will not follow, but will flee from him: for they know not the voice of strangers."

James 4:8 Draw near to God and He will draw near to you. We draw near to Him when we talk to Him one on one. The more we talk and be still, the more we know His voice. Think of someone that is close to you. If they write you a letter, you will hear their voice as you read it. I believe it to be true of God's voice also. You hear His voice in your spirit in all types of instances, whether it is encouragement or conviction. Trust His voice.

I had a ministroke in 2012 and another one in 2017 while in Cusco, Peru studying on a Fulbright-Hays Scholarship. I had skin problems, numerous severe migraines. Between 2017 and 2018, I documented myself having 177 migraines. I had to keep taking prescription migraine medicine for three days for each migraine before the pain went away for good. I had double vision 56 times, dizzy 27 times and my legs gave out and I fell 16 times. Three of those times were here in church. There were two times in which I could not talk for about 30 seconds. I kept falling in class and kept having to leave work early because of migraines. I ended up retiring after teaching for 22 years. In my prayer closet, I heard God tell me that the medicine was killing me. Last year, I wrote in my prayer book: "God help me know when and how to stop taking my medicine.

I did not have a plan. I just asked God to help me. I had a manic episode at the beginning of November. I spent two weeks outpatient and told them that I wanted to get off my medicine. Initially, they tried to prescribe me more medicine. I refused. I began reading about tapering off medicine. I was taking four medications at the time. The doctors helped me taper off two of them in the two weeks and told me to continue taking the remaining two. Eventually, I weaned myself down to one pill that was 375 mg. Last month I was taking 75 mg a day. May 26, 2019, I stopped taking that pill.

Since I got off Lithium, Wellbutrin, Trazodone and Lamictal, I have not fallen once. I have not had double vision. I have not experienced dizziness and I only have an occasional migraine. Since I am retired, I have time to spend two hours if needed in my prayer closet. I have been able to draw nearer to God than ever before. He is my medicine.

Cracks in the Potter's Clay

I ask Him for guidance every day. He helps me to remember to drink plenty of water. He gives me motivation to exercise regularly which helps my mental and physical state. Because of my borderline high cholesterol, He leads me to not have shellfish every time I go out to eat and I do not have to put butter on my popcorn at the movies. I do not make all the right choices but with HIs help, I make better ones.

My prescription in this order is: One on one time with God. I just thank Him for not letting me get any bad news during the night and for salvation and anything else that comes to mind. Then I sing hymns or play them on YouTube. This is how I worship Him. I close my eyes and open the Bible to any book, and I read where my eyes fall. Then I just start talking to Him or read my prayers that I have written down. It starts with please continue to bless me and my loved ones with good health and strength, to continue fighting until the victory is won. I pray for divine protection, mercy, grace, wisdom, guidance, provisions and the desire of our hearts that are good for us.

Then I pray specific prayers with my list of names and groups. I then ask for wisdom, guidance, compassion, patience, forgiveness, strength, understanding, discernment and to use me as He sees fit. I love my Great I Am, Jesus my Savior and Holy Spirit my Comforter."

The Love Feast Meditation that you just read was well received when I read it for the church. I was surprised how many people thanked me for sharing and that they had similar struggles. It seemed to inspire people. It felt good and a little awkward at the same time. What is amazing is that I felt God leading me back then, but it doesn't even compare to where He has brought me to. God had barely scratched the surface of the changes He had in store for me.

God is so very patient. It must have been in 2015 when I came across the scripture: 1 Corinthians 3: 16-17. "Know ye not that ye are the temple of God, and that the Spirit of God dwelleth in you? If any man defiles the temple of God, him shall God destroy; for the temple of God is holy which temple ye are. This scripture convicted me about my long-time habit of smoking cigarettes. I did not smoke everyday but when I did, I would smoke between 1 and four cigarettes. I would mostly only buy loose cigarettes from the corner store for 50 cents each or I would ask for cigarettes from other smokers. I would offer to pay them, but they rarely accepted. Whenever I would buy a whole pack, I would chain smoke until they were gone so that I could start over again and really stop this time.

I had recently joined the free program 1-800-QUIT NOW to stop smoking. I had been working through the workbook and I was on my second stop date because I gave in to temptation out of depression. When I was depressed, I wanted to die anyway so I rationalized that I was getting myself closer to the grave by smoking. It really did not matter to me. When I was not depressed, I would beat myself up for smoking and would just feel awful. I was trying the nicotine patch this time. I was already addicted to nicotine gum. I chewed it for years. I began listening to sleep hypnosis to stop smoking along with binaural beats. I was down to one cigarette a day for about a year. This day, I was in my prayer closet looking for a meditation and I came across a lively preacher who caught my attention.

He said to the congregation that one of his congregants came to speak with him and said: "I just don't know why but I can't stop smoking cigarettes." He told him that the first thing that he had to do was to stop saying out of his mouth that he could not stop smoking. At the time, I kept saying, I cannot give up that one cigarette a day. He told him to stop trying to stop but begin saying; "Thank you Jesus for setting me free from nicotine and cigarettes.: He told him to say it every time he thought about smoking and even while he was smoking a cigarette, he should say it. He said his congregant came back to him in three weeks and said that he had finally stopped smoking. I decided to give it a try.

Every time I thought about a cigarette or smoked a cigarette, I would say: "Thank you Jesus for setting me free from cigarettes and nicotine. Remember, I was addicted to nicotine gum. It felt foolish but I could hear that pastor in my mind saying to not feel guilty about smoking. Just keep saying the words: "Thank you God for setting me free from cigarettes and nicotine. Well, it worked. In about three weeks, I had stopped smoking and had no desire to smoke. I did not suffer from any withdrawal like in the past. I did not overeat. I did not get headaches and I did not feel like I was missing anything. I did, however, develop an intolerance to be around smoke. I never liked the smell of smoke, but it got intensified. The smell of cigarettes on someone's clothes began to make me nauseated or would give me a headache.

I had to distance myself from people who smoked. I had three people in my life who smoked, and I asked them to not smoke in my car or around me. They were great in their support. This time I did not have to ask them to please do not give me a cigarette if I asked them. (It never worked anyway. Lol They could not refrain from giving me one because they were addicted as well and knew what it felt like to want a cigarette and not have one.) I can also be persuasive, and most people did not tell me no. I knew that I was set free. It is now February 3, 2021 and I have not smoked or wanted a cigarette since. Whom the Son sets free is free indeed. John 8:36.

Part II

Chapter 4: I Used to be Full of It!!!

My ex-husband and I were officially separated May 26, 2019, and I was living alone for the first time in my life. I had weaned myself off the last drug. My sister Amina was incredibly happy to hear that I was off all of that medicine and told me that I needed to do a cleanse since I took the drugs for so many years. Amina's mother and my Stepmother, Khadijah, has always been very health conscious and still looks remarkable for her age. Sidebar: Khadijah and I were pregnant at the same time. Me with my firstborn Joshua and her with my twin brothers Hassan and Ali. Khadijah is 10 years older than I and I am 10 years older than Amina. Amina has learned a lot of good habits from her mother. I had never done a cleanse before, but the way Amina described it to me, it sounded like an excellent idea to rid my body of toxins that had built up. We decided to do the 10-Day Green Smoothie Cleanse together.

The daily cleanse consisted of two fruit and vegetable smoothies: one for breakfast and one for lunch and either a salad or grilled vegetables for dinner. The modified dinner could be a piece of lean meat with a salad and vegetables. I chose to do the full cleanse without any meat, dairy, caffeine, sugar, and wheat. The cleanse allowed as snacks a handful of raw unsalted cashews and all the fruits and raw vegetables as desired. I took a natural cleanser in pill form that I had to drink 8-10 glasses of water a day. I drank only water with fresh lemon juice in it for ten days. I would drink hot water in the mornings. When I started the cleanse, I weighed 167 pounds. When I finished the cleanse in 10 days, I was 153 pounds. Day 7 was the most difficult day for me. I felt like crying. My flesh was crying out in distress.

Before the cleanse, my diet consisted of a piece of chicken, fish, or shellfish with every meal, a vegetable and a starch. Occasionally, I would eat ribs. My favourites were buffalo wings (crispy), McDonald's French fries, rock lobster tail, mussels, baked potatoes with butter and sour cream, salads with ranch dressing, cheese pizza, lasagne, greens cooked with smoked turkey meat, and an occasional Wendy's single burger with French fries, chocolate frosty and an occasional double scoop of chocolate chip ice cream from Baskin Robbins. Oh, and do not let me forget the bread. I loved bagels with cream cheese, wheat toast for breakfast, and any restaurant bread. I especially loved Carrabba's Grill bread dipped in olive oil and spices. I sometimes ate pancakes, an occasional Ribeye or Sirloin steak, New England clam chowder, raisin bran cereal, an occasional candy snack of Tootsie Rolls, Peanut Chews or other chocolate. I would eat bacon and eggs occasionally but mostly ate cereal for breakfast or Maple and Brown sugar oatmeal. I would snack on grapes and gala apples because that is what Andre liked. I would eat grilled cheese sandwiches on occasion.

If I went to McDonald's, I would get a fish filet, medium fries and a mocha frappe or a milkshake with vanilla and chocolate mixed. The plain chocolate was too sweet for me. My all-time favourite treat was a Dairy Queen soft serve vanilla cone dipped in chocolate that got hard. (I acquired that addiction on the boardwalk in Ocean City as a child.) I loved lamb chops. I used to drink Cokes, lemonade or coffee with cream and sugar when I went to the movies or out to eat. I also would drink one to two glasses of wine when I went out to eat.

(Maybe twice a month.) I am listing all this so that you can see how drastically my diet changed.

One other thing that I must mention is I used to be chronically constipated. If I did not drink senna tea every day, I could not have a bowel movement. I would go five days without a bowel movement. My mother and sister Adrienne also suffered from constipation. They would always take Correctol laxative, but I did not like it because it made my stomach cramp. This reminds me of a funny story. I was constipated as a teenager and Adrienne was home from college. My mother, Adrienne and I were headed to the Inner Harbor in downtown Baltimore to eat or something. Adrienne gave me an Ex lax laxative bar but cautioned me to only eat a half of one. I told her I was really constipated, and I should take the whole thing. Adrienne begged me not to but I did not listen.

Well, we found parking and was walking through the pavilions and my stomach started to cramp extremely bad. I stopped walking and grabbed my stomach. Adrienne took one look at my face and started laughing hysterically. She said: "I told you Al! Hahahahahaha." I could still hear her laughing as I ran through the pavilion looking for the lady's room. When I found it, there were about 6 ladies in line. I just ran past all of them frantically

Cracks in the Potter's Clay

apologizing and ran into the first door that opened. No one complained that I cut the line. I guess the look on my face let them know the urgency. The ride home was not much better for me. My stomach was still cramping. I was laying across the back seat moaning. My mother was driving, and Adrienne was sitting in the passenger seat laughing at me reminding me that she had warned me.

The 10 Day Green Smoothie Cleanse really changed my life. After the cleanse, I went out to eat and ate some buffalo wings, baked potato with sour cream and butter and a salad. I hated the way my body felt. I felt nauseated and achy. I had injured my back and neck trying to control our two German Shepherds by myself. One pulled me clean off my feet to the ground and the other pulled me down the front stairs. My back hurt so bad when I woke up that I had to do a seven step get it together. It took at least seven steps for me to straighten up on the way to the bathroom in the morning. The doctors also found arthritis in my hand, knee and shoulder. That evening God led me to Google foods that cause inflammation. I did not want to be in pain anymore.

These are the foods that cause inflammation and that I omitted from my diet:

- Dairy
- Meats
- Tomatoes
- Potatoes
- Wheat
- Sugar
- Alcohol
- Bread
- White Rice
- Processed Foods

These are the foods that I stopped because they can trigger migraines:

- Chocolate
- Red Apples
- Almonds
- Alcohol
- MSG
- Hot Sauce
- Hot Dogs
- Raisins
- Grapes
- Processed foods

Avoiding caffeine at all costs: (It keeps me awake and makes me feel uneasy in my mind and body.)

Cracks in the Potter's Clay

I stopped eating shellfish because of what I read in Leviticus about only eating animals from the sea that have scales and fins. I know that the New Testament says that it is not what you put in your body that makes you unclean but what comes out, evil thoughts and speech. But since I was taking Pravastatin for high cholesterol from eating too much shellfish, I decided to stop. I basically eat a piece of salmon for dinner every night. Salmon is good for inflammation. I cook it in different ways for variety.

These are the foods that God has added to my diet that I did not use to like at all:

- Honey (honey is good for you muscles after workouts)
- Mangoes
- Avocados
- Mandarins
- Ginger
- Zucchini
- Squash
- Garlic
- Craisins
- Steel Oats Oatmeal
- Brown Rice

These are the foods that I seldomly used to use but use daily now:

- Pineapple
- Onions
- Olive Oil
- Lemons (I put in water and drink all day long. Lemon juice is particularly good for leg cramps.)

It is especially important to drink this all during the day. I drink at least 48 oz and adding freshly squeezed lemon juice makes it easy for me to drink and the lemon juice builds your immune system.

- Water (Since I moved to Phoenix, I drink 9.5 Alkaline water)

My vegan treats I make from scratch:

Banana nut muffins (I use Vegan alternatives and ¾ cup of honey or agave instead of sugar and butter)

Mix wet and dry ingredients separately first, mix and then scoop batter into mini muffin tins

- 1 ½ cup flour
- 1 ¾ tsp baking soda

- ½ tsp cinnamon
- ¼ tsp salt
- 4 ripe bananas
- ½ cup melted butter
- ½ cup granulated sugar
- ¼ cup brown sugar
- 1 ¼ cup chopped walnuts
- ¼ cup coconut milk or oat
- 1 tsp vanilla extract

Sweet Potato or Pumpkin Pie

Crust: Process together and mash into glass pie dish. No oil needed in dish

- 15-18 pitted dates
- 3 cups of chopped walnuts
- ½ teaspoon cinnamon

Filling:

- 2 large eggs (I use vegan substitutes of ½ banana per egg or milled flaxseed and 1 tbsp of water per egg)
- I cup coconut milk
- I can pumpkin puree or fresh sweet potatoes
- 1 tbsp vanilla
- 2 tsp pumpkin pie spice

Mango and Tumeric Sorbet

- 12 oz frozen mango chunks
- 1 teaspoon grated lime zest
- Juice of ½ lime
- 2 teaspoons ground turmeric
- ½ cup water
- 1 pinch salt
- 5 tablespoons of sugar (I use honey)

Turmeric Tea

First thing in the morning hot drink:
- ½ teaspoon of powdered turmeric
- two tablespoons of honey
- two tablespoons of fresh lemon juice

GInger Tea

Last thing in the evening hot drink:
- ¾ teaspoon of fresh grated ginger
- two tablespoons of honey
- two tablespoons of fresh lemon juice

I sometimes use lime instead of lemon. My diet is particularly good at boosting my **immune system**. The things in my diet that **boost** the immune system are:

Cracks in the Potter's Clay

Lemons, limes, pineapple, olive oil, ginger, avocados, turmeric, mangoes and mandarins

And do not forget **sunlight** is a great source of Vitamin D. I go outside daily.

Chapter 5: The Closet

Writing and self-reflection for me started many years ago. I would have to guess the year 2006. I had just had an operation and was home recuperating. It was quiet in the house. No one home but me. I could not remember the last time that I had been alone for an entire day not to mention two weeks. It hurt to move around so I had brought snacks like fruit in syrup, raisins, sardines, protein drinks and bottled waters upstairs so I would not have to go downstairs for anything. I thought that while I was home, I would do some Bible study and search for scriptures for things that I struggled with. I searched and wrote down scriptures especially for wisdom and anger. These were two areas that I struggled with. I wrote the scriptures under the appropriate headings and began reading them every day. Sometimes I read out loud and sometimes quietly.

Confess Sins First

I thought it was best to confess my sins first. Romans 3:23 states that all have sinned and fallen short of God's grace. 1 John 1:8 states if we say we have no sin, we deceive ourselves and the truth is not in us. But haleluYah 1 John 1:9 states that If we confess our sins, He is faithful and just to forgive us our sins and cleanse us from all unrighteousness. I daily ask God to reveal any unconfessed sins or sins that I am not aware that I committed. He does reveal it to me when I am still salty deep inside about something someone did to me. I practice being cordial to everyone and I do not dwell on offenses but sometimes God lets me know if I have not forgiven completely.

Be Thankful

I want Him to know that I appreciate what He has done for me before I ask for something else. I am so grateful for life and believe that where there is life, there is hope. Reading the following two scriptures everyday help me to focus on God's goodness:

Psalm 107:1 Oh give thanks to the Lord for He is good, and His mercy endures forever.

Psalm 100:4 Enter into His gates with thanksgiving and into His courts with praise. Be thankful unto Him and bless His name. The Lord is good, and His mercy is everlasting. His truth endures through all generations.

Ask For Wisdom

I must share the experience that prompted me to seek God's wisdom. Several years ago, Andre and I were not getting along, and I was feeling depressed. I wanted a cigarette, but I did not have any and it was too late to ask my friend and neighbour Shelly for one. It was probably 1:30 in the morning. Well, let me tell you, when you want to do something wrong, the devil is orchestrating ways for you to do it. The phone rang and it was Michelle telling Andre that their son Jabre had a fever and needed some Tylenol. I volunteered to go to the gas station to get him some and at the same time get myself some cigarettes. Well, I did not like to smoke in the car, so I stood by the store entrance of the gas station and smoked a cigarette. A man came walking up from across the street and asked me if he could have one of my cigarettes. I was glad to oblige him. Smokers love company.

Cracks in the Potter's Clay

I felt extremely lonely when I was depressed. This man listened to me talk while we were smoking. As we finished our cigarettes, he asked me for a ride to the bus stop. I felt it would be ok so I told him yes, but that I had to drop off medicine for my stepson first and that he could ride with me. When we got to Michelle's apartment, the Holy Spirit told me to take my keys out of the ignition and take them with me. I did not recognize His voice back then. I answered myself that if I took my keys the man (whose name I didn't even remember) would think that I didn't trust him, so I left them in the ignition. I had just arrived at her front door when I heard my car peeling off at top speed with my new smoker friend driving.

What made matters even more embarrassing for me, I had left my purse with my wallet, driver's license and credit cards in the back on the floor behind the passenger seat. I did not want to tell Michelle, Andre or anyone else how foolish I was but I had no other choice because I was stranded with no car and Michelle does not drive. I remember her being kind to me and not calling me an idiot which I expected. Andre came and picked me up. He was not as kind as Michelle. He asked me questions that just made me feel worse about myself than I already did. If you have made an unwise decision like I did, reading the following scriptures daily can and will help:

James 1:5 If any man lacks wisdom let him ask of God that giveth to all men liberally and upbraideth not and it shall be given him. But let him ask in faith, nothing wavering for he that wavereth is like the waves of the sea driven with the wind and tossed.

Psalm 19:7 The law of the Lord is perfect, restoring the soul. The testimony of the Lord is true, making wise the simple.

Proverbs 1:5 A wise man will hear and will increase in knowledge and a man of understanding will inquire unto wise counsel.

Proverbs 11:30 The fruit of the righteous is a tree of life and he that winneth souls is wise.

Romans 12:16 Be not wise in your own conceits.

1 Corinthian 4:10 We are fools for Christ's sake but yea are wise in Christ. We are weak but yea are strong ye are honourable but we are despised.

2 Timothy 3:15 And that from a child thou hast known the Holy Scriptures which are able to make thee wise unto salvation through faith which is in Christ Jesus.

Protection

I memorized the Lord's Prayer found in the book of Mathew by reciting it repeatedly with my grandmother Rebecca, great Aunt Ruth and Cousin Edythe. I drove a motorcycle to get around on campus at HU. I was in the habit of saying the Lord's prayer for protection before I kick-started it and drove anywhere. One day, I was riding across campus and a lady stepped into the street in front of me. I made myself spill to prevent hitting her. I just suffered a bruised rib because I was not driving fast. As soon as I picked up my bike, I realized that I had forgotten to pray.

Psalm 91:11 For He orders His angels to protect you wherever you go.

Psalm 91:14 For the Lord says because He loves me, I will rescue him. I will make him great because he trusts in my name.

Faith

My faith which is my driving force stems back to that Easter Sunday searching for Easter eggs when God showed Himself to me and I felt His presence.

All my life since then, I have strived to feel that peace. I will do whatever I have to do to feel that happiness. I felt it so I know it is possible to feel it again. It is what drives my All is on attitude. I have been married three times. That hope inside me made me keep trying to find true love. What I have realized now is that God is my true love. My search is over. He is my everything. These scriptures made it easier for me not to give up:

Psalm 9:15-16 When he calls on me, I will answer. I will be with him in trouble and rescue him and honor him. I will satisfy him with a full life and give him my salvation.

Hebrews 11:16 Without faith it is impossible to please Him, for he who comes to God must believe that He is and that He is a rewarder of those who diligently seek Him.

Hebrews 11:1 Now faith is the substance of things hoped for the evidence of things not seen.

Psalm 6:9 The Lord hath heard my supplication. The Lord will receive my prayer.

Cracks in the Potter's Clay

Anger

Proverbs 14:17 A quick tempered man acts foolishly, and a man of wicked intentions is hated.

Proverbs 16:32 He who is slow to anger is better than the mighty and he who rules his spirit than he who takes a city.

Proverbs 17:27 He who has knowledge spares his words and a man of understanding is of a calm spirit.

I would read these scriptures every day and ask God to help me. It was not intentional, but through repetition, I ended up memorizing all these verses. I did another Love Feast Devotion on a youth Sunday that I would like to share because it had a great influence on me. You see, God speaks to us through His Word. The more time you spend in it, the more revelation you will receive. This Love Feast Devotion was called: The Power of the Tongue.

Proverbs 18:21 Death and life are in the power of the tongue and they that love it shall eat the fruit thereof.

Proverbs 1:5 A wise man will hear and increase in knowledge and a man of understanding will inquire unto wise counsel.

Luke 1: 62-80 Then they made signs to his father to find out what he would like to name his child. He asked for a writing tablet and to everyone's astonishment, he wrote: "His name is John." Immediately his mouth was opened, and his tongue was loosed, and he began to speak, praising God. The neighbours were all filled with awe and throughout the hill country of Judea people were talking about all these things. Everyone who heard this wondered about it, asking, "What then is this child going to be?"

And you my child will be called a prophet of the Most High; for you will go on before the Lord to prepare the way for him, to give his people the knowledge of salvation through the forgiveness of their sins, because of the tender mercy of our God, by which the rising sun will come to us from heaven to shine on those living in darkness and in the shadow of death, to guide our feet into the path of peace. And the child grew and became strong in spirit and he lived in the wilderness until he appeared publicly to Israel.

Cracks in the Potter's Clay

I think that it was beautiful in the Bible days that so much importance was placed on the naming of one's child. The name had significance. Even the community was anxious to know what the child was going to be. Luke 1: 66 says; "What then is this child going to be?" For the Lord's hand was with him.

Proverbs 18:21 states that death and life are in the power of the tongue and they that love it shall eat the fruit thereof. Zechariah in verse 76 said "And you my child will be. And you my child will be." He said it definitively and with authority.

It was his right and responsibility as a parent to profess about his son. A child loves the words of his parents and they will eat the fruit thereof. A parent may say: "My child you will behave in public. You will eat healthy. You will respect your parents. You will have good hygiene. You will respect your teachers. You will study. You will clean up after yourself. You will go to college. You will work. You will save money. You will help others. You will use your gifts to serve God. Zechariah spoke life into his son and the child grew and became strong in spirit.

John the Baptist became everything that his father spoke over him. This is so encouraging to me. As a child becomes older and as we become older, others speak into our lives. It could be positive or negative, so I think it is beneficial for us to pray for wisdom and discernment. Death and life are in the power of the tongue; and they that love it shall eat the fruit thereof. John 10:3-4 Jesus said the watchman opens the gate for him, and the sheep listen to his voice. He calls his own sheep, and he calls them by name and leads them out. When He has brought out all his own, he goes on ahead of them, and his sheep follow him because they know his voice.

A true successful Believer in Christ has a personal relationship with Jesus because in a relationship, you talk to each other and you recognize each other's voices. As a teacher, I learned my students' voices because I heard their voices every day. One of them would talk while my back was turned and I would correct them by name. Sometimes they would deny it was them, but I would tell them that I knew their voice. I think my students appreciated that because it means that they were heard by me. How else could I recognize their voices?

If we spend time in God's word, we will recognize His voice. I have found the Bible to be a living word. By just reading the ten commandments multiple times, you will hear God's voice as you make decisions and live your daily life. Before we make decisions a lot of times God speaks to us and reminds us of His word. He nudges us to do the right thing. We hear his voice, but we do not always listen to it. If we have free will to obey God's voice or not, we can choose whether to receive a negative word someone speaks into our lives. There is power in the tongue.

I found that the scriptures seemed to help. I continued however to have struggles in my relationships. I have discovered that the more you do for people, the more they expect. When I was trying to play the Potter, I would do as much as I could financially and physically for my loved ones. The problem was that I expected appreciation in return. Now I only do what God tells me to do and it is ALWAYS appreciated by the recipient. I had to learn how to love myself first. He had to teach me how to love myself. It was not an easy process. I still had the mindset that the more you do for others, the more you pleased God. I was separated from my husband and my children. Two other close family relationships were also rocky. Once alone in my prayer closet, I started talking to God and He answered.

I did not have anyone else to talk to. I had never lived alone before. I had so much love in my heart with no one to give it to. I felt like everyone hated me and all I was trying to do was love everyone. Once the pity party was over, God showed me my role in the way I was perceived and treated by others. A two-year transformation would begin. He literally made the pot (me) into a new pot. I hold onto the Bible verse Mathew 6:33. Seek ye first the kingdom of God and its righteousness and everything else will be added to you. With the love I had on the inside, I started to share the worship songs that I was listening to in the mornings to brighten people's days. I started doing this after Doris started sending me scriptures every day. Brother Nate during the same time was sending me prayers every day. Both still send them to this day.

Doris and Nate kept disturbing my efforts to stay depressed. They kept bringing my mind back to God. I used to spend weeks in a depressed state in which I did not talk to anyone. If I did talk to anyone it was to complain about my life and how no one loved me. I would sleep a lot in order to escape the feelings of hopelessness. I would be borderline anorexic because I could not eat if I was depressed. Instead, I would smoke cigarettes which also curbed my appetite. I would wait until something happened to perk up my spirits and then I would eat. I found when I exercised, I had a good appetite to eat. Running has always been my best defence for depression. It releases endorphins that make you feel good.

As a teenager, I remember jogging over my Aunt Ruth's house (the one with no mole on her nose). She was a housewife and was home most of the time. My mother, at the time, was at church, the Arena Playhouse or sleeping. I wanted attention. I was feeling lonely. Aunt Ruth was hilarious, and she began to encourage me. It felt so good coming from her because I never felt special to her. You see Adrienne was born on her birthday and she always called Adrienne her birthday girl. I could not compete with that. I wanted to be special too. Well Aunt Ruth finally made me feel special. When I got my drivers' license, my mother would let me borrow her car and I would take Aunt Ruth to Bingo or to the grocery store. I would also take Cousin Edythe places and my neighbour, Mrs. Smith.

Mrs. Smith was a housewife also. I remember wishing that my mother had been a housewife so she would have more time to spend with me. The grass is not always greener on the other side. Now, I cherish every play that my mother was in, every song that she sang, every step that she danced, every sermon that she preached, every one-woman show that she performed for Young Audiences of Maryland and every prayer that she prayed. Les Brown says, "Some things are taught, and some things are caught." What my mother did not teach me, I caught by watching her. I even remember watching her praise the Lord when I would go to church with her. I find myself mimicking her gestures. It is almost like I feel her within me. She nurtured all my interests as a child. That costs money. She worked to provide opportunities for me.

If she had not worked, I would not have attended Private Catholic Schools nor been able to enjoy a summer home in Ocean Pines, MD. I was so thankful that she was a teacher because I had her on weekends, holidays and all summer long. Some of my favourite memories are of my mother singing to me on the 3-hour trip to Ocean Pines. She would sing a variety of West Indian songs and songs she learned performing when she was in college. When the electricity would go out due to a storm in Ocean Pines and even at our home in Baltimore, she would sing the voodoo song Rah Cum Bay to scare us. We would say: "Mommy, sing Rah Cum Bay!" We would scream and be scared every time. Lol Another great one with different languages was called Everybody Loves Saturday Night.

As you can see, my mother gave me a lot of attention and quality time. It helped shape me into the woman that I am today. My stepfather, Joseph Louis Coursey, had a big influence on the woman that I became also. I honestly believe my Bipolar 1 was triggered when he and my mother decided to separate, and he left the house. We called him 'Pop'. Pop was albino and was legally blind. He had blonde hair that was the texture of a soft bush, but he only had hair around the sides and back. No hair on top. He always wore fishing style hats to cover his bald head and to protect himself from the sun. Albino people's skin is overly sensitive to the sun. People used to call him Blondie. Some called him Bozo like the clown. He was teased as a child.

As a matter of fact, his own mother took one look at him when he was born, saw that he was albino and left him in the hospital stating: "That ain't no baby of mine." His grandmother, Lucymae, went to the hospital and got him and raised him. He grew up with the knowledge that his mother did not want him and always wanted her acceptance. I met her on a couple of occasions. He took it extremely hard when Grandma Lucymae died. I had met her also. She was sweet. I think my mother told me this about him early on. He was an alcoholic and I believed it was because of the pain he suffered being rejected by his mother and teased all his life. I remember feeling sorry for him and deciding to love him. My grandfather influenced this decision. Well, a story my mother told me at the age of four when my maternal grandfather died.

My mother's father, Isaiah Johnson, died when he was 78 years old of cancer. He had the brightest, warmest smile that I have ever seen on a man. I remember him bringing us animal crackers to the house when he came to visit. I remember seeing him standing in the kitchen with the bag of animal crackers in his hand. I remember how I felt when he came around. I felt warm. I was born the day before his birthday. His birthday was April 6th. I wish that I could have waited one more day because I thought he was so special. On his deathbed, my mother told me that he sang this song: 'What the world needs now is love sweet love. That's the only thing that there's just too little of. What the world needs now is love sweet love, no not just for sone but for everyone. '

Yes. I decided to love Pop. He must have felt it because he became the first man to make me feel loved. His birthday was October 8th. He was a Libra. The Libra sign is the scales. That never seemed relevant to me until just a few months ago. I became close friends with my neighbour Leon who is a Libra. When he moved to the neighbourhood with his wife Pat and children

Cracks in the Potter's Clay

Allison and Patrick, I was a teenager. Over the years we would have a conversation on the sidewalk when we happened to get home at the same time.

Three months before my divorce from Andre was final. I became involved with one of the handymen that was doing work for me. He was a Libra. I liked the way he talked to me. Unfortunately, I thought that he was a true child of God walking in truth, but he was only pretending to take advantage of me financially. He was much younger than me and said that he wanted to marry me. He said he wanted me to do ministry back in his country. He worked so hard for me and was so charming that I believed him. Two months and 12,000 in credit card debt later, I found out that he was a scammer. My neighbour Leon caught me on the sidewalk when I was happy in this relationship and he was happy for me.

When God put an end to the relationship by opening my eyes, I reached out to Leon who is older and wiser than I. He seemed to be able to explain to me about blind spots and helped encourage me and help me to heal after the hurtful relationship.

Leon and I became closer friends, and I had a newfound love for cooking healthy meals and Leon had a love to eat my healthy meals. In conversation, I asked him when his birthday was. He told me it was October 13th. Wow. That is the same day as my long-time friend, co-worker and Taekwondo instructor's birthday. They were even born in the same year. I thought that it was remarkably interesting that the man I was going to marry, Leon and Edward are all Libra men. Then, I realized my ex-husband Andre and my friend Andre Cooper is also a Libra! Mr. Cooper and I were close and had been weekly running partners for years. We even worked together one summer at the karate school summer camp and we co-taught cardio classes. We ran every Saturday and would go pig out afterwards.

It amazes me that Edward, Andre Cooper and Leon and I have positive, mutually respectful relationships with each other. I find all of them intelligent, funny and supportive. I was married to an Aquarian for 10 years and a Gemini for 21 years. According to Astrology which I did not base my decisions on was who I was supposed to be compatible with. I am an Aries and are highly compatible with Libra. All I have to say is that God supplies all my needs. My friendships are important to me. I have decided to remain divorced and do the work of the Lord. I hear His voice more clearly living alone and I am very content.

I find it more than interesting that I am Bipolar 1 and experience extreme ups and downs and that I have long standing friendships with Libra men. I do not live my life according to astrology and I did not seek these men out because they were Libra. I just know that when I am around them, I feel balanced. Most men are afraid to tell me no for some reason. They do not want to upset me. My stepfather was strict and stern. I was afraid of him, so I did everything he said to do. He taught my sister and I how to clean and we received allowance for doing our weekly chores. My Taekwondo instructor, Mr. Edward Bryant, was a strict and disciplined trainer. I grew extraordinarily strong while training under him. My running partner, Mr. Cooper would push me also. Leon is also a great accountability partner.

The Power of the Holy Spirit

One major difference in my life spiritually is the presence and power of the Holy Spirit within me. All the preachers that God led me to on Facebook spent time discussing the Holy Spirit. Ever since I was saved at age 17, I prayed to God the Father and Jesus the Son. Now I also pray to the Comforter who is the Holy Spirit and have received power. I have never been so clear on His guidance. I used to trust in medicine to regulate my moods and to help me sleep. Now I am led by the Spirit. He guides my daily activities.

Being retired and living alone has made it a lot easier to hear Him. Not having to wake up at a certain time, I allow myself to wake up naturally. As soon as my eyes open, I say: "Thank you God for waking me up and not letting me get any bad news during the night." I ask Him to order my steps in HIs word and I ask the Holy Spirit to have his way in my life and to guide my thoughts, words and actions. I would then pick up my phone and look on Facebook. It seemed like as soon as I reached Facebook, a preacher would have just started preaching or teaching and it always seemed as if they were talking directly to me. I found great comfort in this.

I realized that the news and programs that I used to watch like Law and Order, Perry Mason and Murder She Wrote began to unsettle me. People are murdered every day. Philippians 4:4-9 Rejoice in the Lord always. I will say it again: Rejoice! Let your gentleness be evident to all. The Lord is nearby. Do not be anxious about anything, but in every situation, by prayer and petition, with thanksgiving, present your requests to God. And the peace of God, which transcends all understanding will guard your hearts and your minds in Christ Jesus. Finally, brothers and sisters, whatever is true, whatever is noble, whatever in right, whatever is pure, whatever is lovely, whatever is admirable-if anything is excellent or praiseworthy-think about such things. Whatever you have learned or received or heard from me or seen in me-put it into practice. And the God of peace will be with you.

One of the traits of Bipolar 1 is depression. When I got depressed, it felt like a dark cloud came and hovered over my head and poured heaviness and hopelessness on me to the point I could not be productive. All I wanted to do is isolate myself and smoke cigarettes or drink wine and go to sleep. The depression was usually triggered by something. Once, I was at a women's church retreat and it was the last night. For fun they played music and had dancing. I had outlasted everyone on the floor when a particular song came on. This song immediately triggered a teenage memory of one of my boyfriends who had taken advantage of me and broke my heart. I stopped dancing and began to weep. I was so embarrassed that I could not control the mood swing that I got my things and left without saying goodbye to anyone.

I then did what I regularly did when I felt depressed; I went outside in search of a smoker to bum a cigarette from. I know it was self-destructive to smoke and that is why it seemed so appealing. When the depression overtook me, I wanted to die anyway. I saw smoking as a means to an end; to get me closer to death. I usually did not buy packs of cigarettes because I was always trying to stop smoking and I did not feel the need to smoke all the time. Unfortunately, my mind would not let me have a pack of cigarettes in my possession and just smoke one when I wanted one. If I bought a pack, I found myself trying to hurry up and smoke them so that I could quit again. I have given and thrown away hundreds of packs of cigarettes to keep from smoking them.

When I felt depressed, I felt that the way things were at that time was how they were always going to be. If things were bad, they were going to stay bad. I did not have hope. I felt powerless to change any situations so I would resort to self-destructive behaviour. It was something that I could control. I felt that no one understood me, and no one really appreciated me. Little did I realize that I did not understand or appreciate myself. In my mountaintop experience with God, (alienated from my closest relatives) He started to teach me about myself. He first started speaking to me through worship songs that I would find on YouTube.

James 4:8 Draw near to God and He will draw near to you. I felt alone and I found that when I focused on praising God, the depression would leave. I then started sharing the songs that lifted my spirit up to people on my contact list on my phone. Some people would respond, and it encouraged me to continue but I did not do it every day. Doris sending me Bible scriptures and prayers every day taught me how to be consistent. That is what I 'caught' from Doris. God dwells in consistency.

Chapter 6: The Fight/The Flesh

I have always liked physical activities and competing. I would often focus on one sport for a while until I reached a proficiency that showed I could master it if I wanted and then I would move on to something else. It seems that I like challenges. They say that an idle mind is the devil's workshop. The times that I used to be depressed were never when I was focusing on something physical. I would get depressed when I was doing nothing but thinking about the present situation. When I realized that I could not change the situation, I would self- medicate by sleeping, smoking cigarettes and on some occasions drinking wine. Once I totally surrendered to God and let the Holy Spirit lead me, He taught me the importance of overcoming the flesh. In my case, the battle of the mind.

Joyce Meyer's book *Battlefield of the Mind* gave me powerful techniques for fighting Satan; all based on the Bible and practical examples. I highly recommend it. I was reading it every day on Facebook and YouTube in order to encourage others. I stopped doing it because my long-time childhood neighbour and friend, Peggy told me that I could be sued because I did not have Joyce Meyer's permission. I was simultaneously doing a Spanish devotion on YouTube with a Spanish version of one of Joel Olsteen's books. I had to go back and delete days and days of videos that I had posted. I am so glad that God has placed people in my life to help me. He has sent me people that genuinely care about me. It is easier to take criticism or instruction from someone that you know cares about you. God provides for us through others.

A Familiar Face Comforted Me

The night before my social security disability hearing, I was extremely nervous. I had been denied benefits three times already. I had already retired from teaching under disability, but that money would not be enough to sustain all my bills and expenses for two homes. I was separated from my third husband at the time and we both took our own bills, so my financial support was cut in half. During this wilderness time, I learned to seek God instead of worry. When I could not fall asleep, I opened my phone to YouTube and came across a sermon by Priscilla Shirer. I absolutely loved her in the movie War Room. The sermon really uplifted my spirit and I fell asleep. My cousin Judy agreed to accompany me to my hearing for emotional support. I was nervous until I walked in and saw that the judge looked just like Priscilla Shirer!

Judy recalled the first thing the judge said when we were seated was that she found my case very compelling. I did not even hear her say that. You see, my back was hurting extra bad when I got to the hearing. I had to ask the judge if it was alright for me to stand up because the sitting was causing me so much pain. I was in more pain than usual. I believe God allowed my pain to be visible for the judge to ensure my approval this time. It was also based on my diagnosis of Bipolar 1 and my four hospitalizations due to manic episodes. Also considered were my chronic migraines, dizziness, double vision and falls from muscle weakness. Before I left the courtroom, I told the judge that she reminded me of my favourite actress and preacher, and she said that she considered that an honour.

Cracks in the Potter's Clay

I received my favourable decision within a few weeks. God's timing is amazing. Soon after the hearing while praying in my closet, God spoke to me and told me that the medicine was killing me. He then showed me how to wean off of it and what to do to replace it. He told me to run at least one mile every day, swim once a week, and get in the sauna daily. These activities help to relieve my arthritic inflammation expel much of my energy so that I would be tired enough to sleep well. Proper rest is key for people with Bipolar 1 as well as for everyone. I ended up purchasing my own two-person sauna from Amazon. I made it a habit to spend an hour a day in 140 degrees while I read my 25-page prayer book.

A Hurtful Truth That Changed My Life

Sheila is a good friend. I was her personal trainer and we continued to train and eat together outside of the gym. We have developed Bestie status. One day, I was very unhappy with my family life and I vented to Sheila for a long time. She did not say anything that evening. She waited until we went out to dinner the following week and proceeded to tell me how I drained her, and how she felt horrible after she left my presence. I did not know what to say. Tears were streaming down my cheeks. I wanted to crawl under the table and hide. It hurt me that she did not tell me at the time but waited until I was happy. I did not call her for a couple weeks, but I kept thinking about what she said. I do not ever want to bring people down. I only want to lift people up. Now, I mostly vent to God. He can handle it.

Chapter 7: Trust Him with The Dance of Your Life

I learned to trust God with my life through a dance. My dear childhood friend Marion's daughter Geanine passed away at the young age of 26 on February 26, 2019. My sister Adrienne called me and told me. I remember God leading me to go to the grocery store and buy certain things to take over her house. When I got there, she was not there but I remember texting her that I would leave them on the porch. Well, I started down the front steps and she pulled up in her black jeep. I was so relieved to see her. She couldn't park fast enough, and I couldn't run to her fast enough. We just stood in the middle of the street holding each other and crying. Later in the house, it came up that she wanted two dancers for Geanine's memorial service. She wanted her service to be special.

I told Marion that I had been dancing with a dance ministry named after my mother and I would love to dance at Geanine's memorial. Marion shared with me how my mother had influenced her life as a child. I was amazed at the specific memories she shared about my mother that helped shape her life to be a self-sufficient and powerful woman. I had fallen in love with the song: Hills and Valley by Tauren Wells at least one month earlier. It moved me deeply the first time that I heard it and every time afterwards. I recalled wanting to dance to it but knew our choreographer Angela Smith chose our anointed songs for the Rev. Joan Coursey Sign and Dance Ministry. I pulled the song up on YouTube and played it for Marion to see if she liked it. She wept and said "That's the one Al."

I thought that it would be easy to make up the dance since I had already fallen in love with the song. It truly ministered to me during my wilderness experience in the valley. The song is about God being God over the hills and the valleys and that He gives and takes away. The melody was so beautiful that it made it easier to accept the lyrics which were to ultimately trust God in the good times and the bad times. I have choreographed dances for myself in the past. I had no idea that this dance would be drastically different.

Cracks in the Potter's Clay

The night I decided to get started on the dance, I did my warmup and played the song so that I could feel the steps as they usually would come. Well, as soon as I tried to choreograph the first step, my knee started hurting. It was the knee that I had surgery on in September of 2018. It had healed and I had not been experiencing any pain for a couple months. It hurt so bad that I had to stop and grab it. I waited a few minutes, started the song over, thought of a step to begin and began to dance the step I envisioned. The pain in my knee was excruciating. I could not believe it, but I could not dance. I felt God telling me to trust Him for the steps. I went upstairs and wrote down the words to the song and practiced singing it.

The next day, I tried to make up steps to it again. My head can be extremely hard. Well, the same thing happened, and I could not bear the pain. I knew God was telling me to trust Him. I listened to the song every day. At least one other time when I felt a great move, I jumped up to practice the move and the pain in my knee would not allow me to execute the move. I became frustrated and laid down. I know God knew my thoughts, but I did not talk to Him about it because of my respect for Him. I was feeling that it was not fair to make me get up in front of a church full of people without having practiced the dance. I recall pouting about it.

I remember calling Marion the night before the memorial and explaining to her that I did not know what steps I was going to do. I was so extremely nervous. She knew exactly what to say. She said that if I got up in front of the church and all I did was spin around in circles, she would be happy. This statement from her took all my fear away. After all, I was doing it for Marion so if she was happy, why should I be nervous. That was an incredibly low expectation. I knew that I would be able to do more than spin around in circles. I am a trained dancer thanks to my mother's sacrifice in paying for my ballet, tap and jazz lessons as a teenager and lessons with Maria Broom when I was a little girl. I got to the church at least an hour early in order to stretch. I had already gone to the gym and spent time in the sauna while stretching. I was too stiff, and my back would hurt too much to dance without going to the sauna first. I rushed from the sauna to the church in order to stretch and keep my muscles warm before I danced.

I stood at the back of the church stretching and watching the memorial service. It was beautiful. I followed along on the program to make sure I would be ready. It was time. I stood in the back of the church waiting to be introduced. I was nervous so I closed my eyes and said, "God use me as your vessel and help me Mommie." While my eyes were still closed in prayer, I heard my introduction, and it blew me away in a good way. On the program it read as follows:

Liturgical Dance...........................Allison Hall-Pridgen
(Rev. Joan Coursey Dance Ministry)

What the preacher said was: "And now we will have a liturgical dance from Reverend Joan Coursey." I was totally psyched to hear my mother's name. I just took off running down the aisle, reached the end in perfect timing to dance to the first words. The Holy Spirit led me through the entire dance, cartwheel and all. I never felt so free and happy in all my life. When I finished, I had also never been so exhausted.

I ran 200-yard dashes and was never so out of breath as when I danced that day. I was embarrassed having people watch me walk back to the back of the church where my seat was because I was breathing so hard. When I sat down, I continued to breathe heavily. It felt like I was hyperventilating. Someone brought me a glass of water. What was even more amazing; the lady sitting in front of me turned and asked me if I was Joan Coursey's daughter.

I proudly said "Yes." She proceeded to tell me that she knew my mother very well and had worked with her for years at Harlem Park Elementary School in Baltimore City. She told me how much she loved my mother. It was music to my ears that my mother was remembered so fondly. If the pastor had not introduced me the way she did, that conversation and connection would not have happened. All things work together for good for those who love God and who are called according to His purpose. Romans 8:28. My sister Adrienne videotaped the dance from her seat at the front of the church. I was amazed when I saw the video because I did dance moves that I had never done before. It was as if it was not me dancing. I got the help that I asked for when I prayed. I felt my mother.

From the first dance Hills and Valleys, the Holy Spirit has led me through 6 more dances. The last one was on my mother's birthday which was February 8, 2020. Each dance is different, and I prepared the same way for each. I wrote the lyrics down and listened to the song over and over. I did condition ballet workouts, but I never practiced one step before the dances. I am going to put all the names of the dances at the back of the book in case you would like to go watch any of them. I give God all the glory. I know He is the one who led me, and they even serve as encouragement for me when I need it. He will come through if you do not doubt Him.

I didn't always feel wanted. I believe that is why Danny Gokey's song 'Wanted' made me cry the first time that I heard it. Through surrendering to God's will, He showed me that I was indeed wanted. I am wanted by Him to spread the good news of Jesus Christ and to encourage others to walk by faith. 'Wanted was the 6th song that I danced to solely under the anointing of the Holy Spirit with no memorized choreography. I did not realize that I was holding my breath while I was dancing, (I had been swimming a lot and I like to swim the length of the pool underwater at the end of my workout.) I remember feeling exhausted and saying to myself: "What are you going to do now? You have used all of your energy." Well, praise God as soon as I thought that God cut the music off for me so that I could catch my breath. I just stood there and breathed for a minute. Then I continued the dance without music, and it ministered to people. He does not just want us; He wants the best for us. He wants to take care of us and provide our every need. I needed to rest, and He gave it to me. The 7th and last dance I did to the song: "Fix Me Jesus" was the dance that I was not even nervous about. I knew God had my back.

Chapter 8: The Call to Phoenix, AZ

I went to visit Christina, Gabriel aka Charlie and my granddaughter, Kameha for the second time for Christmas. I stayed from December 15, 2020 to December 30, 2020. While on my flight, I was able to count back to see when my online ministry began in Baltimore and it began June 7, 2019. I have done a live devotion on YouTube every single day on which I give thanks to God, sing a hymn, read the Bible, take communion and pray. I was also doing a Facebook live Prayer Run a few days a week. On the Prayer Run, I take my German Shepherd, Nikita, for a one to two mile run while I am videotaping live on Facebook. I noticed names appearing even when people did not comment.

For example, it will say at the bottom of the screen; Douglas Marrow is watching. I personally knew all my Facebook friends until I joined Les Brown's Power Voice System and began getting friend invites from like-minded individuals. When I get the invites, I look at their pages before I accept the friendship and if I see positive, Godly posts, I accept. When the names pop up, (who God shows me is watching and in need of prayer) I pray for them. I also encourage viewers to exercise, speak life and to trust God. Well, when I visited Christina for Christmas, I did a Facebook live Prayer Run every morning before Christina left for work. I began to reflect on this fact when I returned to Baltimore. I flourished spiritually while in Phoenix for Christmas. I was also welcomed by Kameha's family and Christina's friends. I felt loved...wanted.

Some other things that I thought about when I returned to Baltimore from Phoenix was my daily sauna ritual. The heat helps relieve stiffness and pain in my body from Arthritis until God ultimately takes it away. I thought about the fact that the only person I saw consistently was Heather, my friend and hair stylist. My son, Joshua also lives in Phoenix. It felt so good to hold my granddaughter. She is a loving child. While in Phoenix, my daughter and Charlie treated me very well. They showed that they appreciated me. For years I longed to feel appreciated by my immediate loved ones. My daughter took such good care of me that I gained five pounds during my trip because she was cooking or buying me all kinds of wonderful vegan meals. Instead of going on a date my last night there, they chose to take me out.

These thoughts kept running through my mind. I did mention to my daughter that I did enjoy Phoenix and asked if she had a problem if I decided to move to Phoenix in the future. She said that she did not mind but ultimately, she would like to get out of Phoenix in the summertime because of the extreme heat. The day she arrived in Phoenix for the first time, it was 124 degrees. She remembers that because she had just driven her car packed with everything that she owned in it for four days and 124 are her birthday numbers. Her birthday is January 24th. I was just thinking about it, but I didn't feel compelled to move to Phoenix. Well, God had other plans.

I believe it was February 16, 2021 that I received a call from my daughter asking if I would move to Phoenix to help with my granddaughter because the other person who was going to start watching her got her dream job. She said she needed me like yesterday. I told her ok. She told me that she would start looking for an apartment for me. That was exactly one month ago today. Today is March 16, 2021 and I am writing this book on my computer in my one-bedroom apartment in Phoenix. I told my daughter that she hears from God because this is the perfect apartment for me. It has a pool, I am on the first floor, it is quiet, and I am within two blocks of every store and service that I would ever need. My dog Nikita is with me. What an adventure the trip was.

I pray every day to be anxious for nothing, so I was kind of taking my time from the 16th when Christina asked me to come to the 22nd when I realized how badly she needed me. I called Christina on Messenger video. Well, Christina was at work with Kameha! I was shocked. I had felt the Holy Spirit nudging me for days that I didn't have to take my time, but I didn't take the hint. Seeing Christina with the baby at work triggered something in me. I thought to myself; She reaaaalllllllyyyyy needs me! Marion had already provided me with a storage bin for the top of my car. I did not even have to ask her for it. When she found out I was moving, she called and told me that I could go and get it from our friend Monica. I picked it up on the 20th.

God provides for HIs children through His children. I had only packed a few things when I spoke to Christina that Monday afternoon. After that phone call, I went into overdrive. I requested help from my dear friend and neighbour Leon to help me with the storage bin called an X-cargo. Well, Leon not only helped me pack that, but he also helped me load everything in my car and cleaned everything. I wanted to leave the upstairs clean in order to utilize it as another Airbnb that could offset my cost for my new apartment. As I was packing, Leon was loading the car. Around 9:00 pm, I called Alvester, my dear friend and herbalist, to see if he could prepare some herbs for my German Shepherd Nikita because she gets car sick. The more I packed, the more energy I got. My mania was in full throttle.

I knew that I would not be able to sleep that night, so I decided to leave. Leon told me later that he did not believe me when I said that I was going to leave that night. He said he did not believe me until he looked out of his window and my car was gone. I went to Alvester's house to get the herbs and say my goodbyes to another dear friend. Alvester also shared his knowledge with me of dog training. He has made herbs for most of my loved ones with desired results. He is that anointed and gifted.

Nikita is especially important to me. I always say that we are each other's service animals. Her with her chemical imbalances and me with mine. Bipolar 1 people are very impulsive. She is a big

Shepherd, weighing in at 90 lbs, with a big bark. No one messes with me when she is with me. I can go jogging at night-time and when people see us coming, they cross over to the other side of the road. Leon has a great mind. He was able to fit everything I needed into my SUV. I could not have done that. He lowered the back of the front seat back and we put Nikita's bed next to me in the front seat. I had a strap attached to her collar attached to the seat belt in case we were in an accident. I did not want her to fly through the windshield.

Thank God for the Waze navigation system. It not only tells you the fastest route, but if there is a car on the side of the road, a police officer up ahead or a quicker alternate route. The longest I have ever driven was 8 hours. I sometimes would drive to Hampton, VA and back to Baltimore, MD on the same day. What drove me to know that I could make this trip was my competitiveness. Christina made the drive in four days. Douglas, my ex, made the drive in three days. I would beat them both. Lol. It is just how God made me. The more I seek His guidance, the more He shows me that my disability is a superpower when I allow Him to lead me. If I lead myself, the symptoms are disabilities.

Alvester gave me two bottles of herbs for Nikita. One to relax her and help her sleep and one to settle her stomach. The only problem is he told me to put it in water, but she was not thirsty. We rode about 30 minutes when she threw up for the first time. She proceeded to throw up for eight hours. Our first stop was in Cumberland, MD. I stopped at a McDonald's to use the bathroom, but the inside was closed to the public. I then found a gas station thanks to my Waze. I was so grateful for Leon because one of the last things he did before we left was to get Nikita's long leash I had attached to my front steps. I fastened the leash around a pole and Nikita used the bathroom while I went inside to use the bathroom and buy something to keep me awake.

I then proceeded to a Marriott hotel and parked in front of the hotel. I cleaned the car as best I could. Most of the vomit was on the edge of her bed and on the door. I was able to wipe it off and put it in a plastic trash bag. We took our first nap at 3:30 am. I woke up an hour and a half later and got back on the road. Our next stop was in PA to get gas. I tied her to a pole and went inside to use the restroom. I did not waste any time. As big and ferocious as Nikita looks, she is friendly, and I thought that someone might steal her. I love her and know that no one will take as good care of her as I do.

Cracks in the Potter's Clay

She continued to throw up but would not drink the water with the herbs in it. Out of frustration to give her the herbs, I took the dropper, pried her mouth open and squeezed the bitter herbs into her mouth. I noticed she began to relax in about an hour. She was not sleeping well at all. It was like she could not get comfortable. When the herbs kicked in, she began to relax and sleep. I was so glad. She was looking so pitiful. I would just rub her head and tell her what a good girl she was. Al had told me to only feed her snacks for the duration of the trip and assured me that she would not starve. Well, Nikita decided not to even eat the snack I bought her. She only drank water whenever we stopped.

I suppose it was around the 8th hour of us driving and I began hearing a loud noise. I looked in the sunroof and the side of the X-cargo was ajar. There was a latch in the front and one in the back. I pulled over on the side of the road and the back latch had completely come open. I was very thankful that none of my things flew out on the highway and caused an accident. It was a little nerve racking trying to close the latch because big, loud trucks were speeding by and making me nervous. I had no choice but to finish. I just prayed for God to protect us. After attaching the latch, I got back in the car and used Waze to find the nearest Walmart to try to find something to tie around the storage bin to keep it shut.

There was a Walmart three miles away. I was so grateful. I am glad that it was February and not August because I had to leave Nikita in the car. If it were hot, I would not have wanted to leave her in the car. I had no idea what to buy. Monica had mentioned that they had used bungee cords but how would I be able to get them around that big bin? I said a silent prayer and asked God to help me. I found an associate and described my dilemma. He told me that I needed to buy ratchet straps. He helped me pick them out and told me that he would come to my car and help me. I did not even have to ask him for help.

As we walked to the car I said, "God always puts a ram in the thicket." I was pleasantly surprised when he said; "Yes. He does. His name was Bryan. I am going to stop writing now in order to add him to my daily prayer list before I forget. The straps he told me to get were too long so he said that we will go back and exchange them for the shorter ones. He patiently waited for me and then returned to the car and secured one towards the front and one towards the back. I did not have much money, but I gave him 5 dollars for his help. I knew he was not doing it for the money, so I just put it in his pocket and said thank you. Sometimes if you extend money to someone, they will not take it. I needed to bless him. So, I did.

The first two days we drove until we needed gas and we also would stop at the rest stops and rest. For close to two years, God has been my alarm clock. I trust Him to wake me up when I am rested enough. I did the same thing on the road. The third day was the most difficult. I was very tired, and I could not make it to the rest stops before I got sleepy. Sometimes, I would make a Facebook live and sing songs to entertain myself and my dear Facebook friends and followers who were virtually following my trip. I was still praying for the names that God showed me and many prayers were being lifted for me. It was very encouraging to me to know that people were praying for us and wishing us well. I was the one always praying for others and now so many people whom I did not even know were supporting me.

Driving through New Mexico was challenging. It was the beginning of the third day, and I was exhausted. I was low on gas and passed a gas station, but it was on the other side. I drove for about 10 miles hoping for another gas station but to no avail. I hated to double back but I turned around and drove back to the gas station that I had passed. It was all desert, and I did not want to run out of gas. There were not even any streetlights on the road. I was stinking and so was Nikita. I tied her up and went inside and bought some deodorant, toothpaste, toothbrush and a yellow Route 66 T-shirt. Leon packed my stuff so well; I knew I would not be able to put it back the way he had packed it. I washed up in the bathroom using paper towels and hand soap.

I felt better but as I was approaching the exit, I heard Nikita barking. I came outside and she was barking at another dog. I got her and put her in the car. I reached for my phone so that I could start the Waze again and I could not find my phone. I got out of the car and walked over to where I tied up Nikita. No phone. I then retraced my steps inside and asked the cashiers if they had seen my phone. Nope. I tried the car again and then asked the cashier if she would call my phone. My heart started beating a little fast because I was in the middle of the desert in a strange land with no directions. I quickly whispered a prayer and thought of the worst-case scenario. I would have to buy a new phone. I had enough money if needed. I took a deep breath and relaxed.

I ran out to the car while she was calling my phone and praised the Lord because it was underneath

Nikita. It seems that whenever I surrender to His will whether it be good or bad, God works things out for me. It seems He tests me regularly to see if I will trust Him through any circumstance. Like Paul in the Bible, I have learned to be content in any situation. Glory to God.

I made a total of eleven Facebook live videos while on the road. I left Baltimore, MD Monday, February 22nd at 12:00 am and arrived in Phoenix Thursday, February 25th at 1:00pm. I was so surprised to just see the last live prayer run I posted on the 26th had 468 views. Before my trip, I was averaging 100 views on my Facebook lives. God had sent people to pray my way across the country. The last 24 hours were the hardest. I was so tired and was only averaging a few hours of driving at a time. I kept getting sleepy and had to pull over on the side of the road. I felt people praying for me.

I made the live videos on the road initially to continue my daily ministry of praying for people. It became so much more. I would sing on the videos to help to distract me and keep me awake. I would testify of God's goodness and provisions He made for me on the road. I noticed many total strangers posting prayers for my and my dog's safety. It was amazing. I am feeling emotional while typing this because knowing that people were praying for me really did strengthen me and let me know that God would not forsake me no matter how tired I felt. The videos also serve as a record of my trip. I am so incredibly grateful.

The Name Change

My divorce was final on September 21, 2021. I decided to go back to my previous name, not my maiden name. My previous name was Allison Joan Hall. I kept my first husband Douglas' last name because we were married when we had our children and I always wanted to have the same name as my children. You want to hear something you may find silly? My reasoning for keeping the name Hall after I divorced was in case one of the children got hurt in school and was rushed to the hospital, I did not want to be denied seeing them because we did not share the same name. I did not want to have to take time to prove I was their mother. Our last names will always be the same. Even though they are adults now, motherhood is an especially important part of my identity. I take pride in that.

I changed my name on my driver's license on February 2, 2021 before I left Baltimore and had planned on changing my social security card and on my bills soon after. Well, I got distracted and no longer treated changing my name as a priority. I was satisfied just having my drivers' license changed. I was focusing on furnishing my apartment and taking care of my granddaughter. Mind you, I am praying every day for God to order my steps in HIs word and for the Holy Spirit to guide my thoughts, words and actions. The only time during the last two years that I did not read my multiple page prayer book was when I was driving to Phoenix.

I had forgotten it in my sauna in Baltimore and Leon was kind enough to go get it for me and mail it to me. I believe it was my third day in Phoenix when I received a call from Cashapp that my account was compromised. The Holy Spirit tried to warn me when I got the recording to just hang up. I just figured; I would not give my social security number. They knew that I was traveling and other information that made me think it was legitimate.

They did not need that in order to scam me. I gave them other information that allowed them to clean out my checking account in small amounts. My bank ended up crediting me the money, but they had to deactivate that card. Since I had to order a new card, I made an appointment to bring my divorce decree and drivers' license in to change my name on the account and my address while I was at it. Since then, I have changed my mailing address at the post office and just about all my correspondence. Had I not been scammed; I would still be Allison Hall-Pridgen on most documents. Since, I did not lose anything, I can see God's hand and not the devil as I initially thought. All things work together for good for those who love God and are called according to His purpose. Romans 8:28

Closure: Marriage Number Three

Since the divorce, Andre and I have been able to maintain a positive friendship and I am incredibly grateful for that. I got my closure last week when he called for assistance because he was buying a house with his closest cousin and needed proof that he was not liable for my house. He had signed the quick claim deed giving me the premarital house back. He needed proof from my insurance of how much I paid. We had two three-way conversations with both the insurance and the mortgage companies. When we finished the call and he had gotten what he needed, I could hear the happiness in his voice, and it stirred up emotions within me. I still love him and liked making him happy. I always did like to make him happy. He did not know it, but I got off the phone and wept bitterly. I tried to reach my therapist but could not. I tried to call Sheila but she was busy.

I called Leon and explained to him what had happened. I could not understand why I was crying so hard. Leon made me feel so much better. He told me that it was normal to grieve the 21-year relationship and that something would be wrong with me if I did not grieve the marriage. Twenty-one years is a long time and that him buying a new home was the closure I needed to trigger the grief. I was in a new state. We both were moving forward. I tell you, Les was right when he said that you can not see the frame when you are in the picture. I so appreciate my friendships that can offer me a different perspective.

Chapter 9: My Miracles

This chapter is based on my favourite scripture; Psalm 37:4 Delight yourself in the Lord and He will give you the desires of your heart.

I say this scripture so much on my Facebook live prayer run when I am encouraging people. I delight myself in Him in many ways. I delight myself in Him by being thankful for all His blessings, by worshipping Him in song and dance, by praying to Him for myself and others and by accepting His will for my life, whatever it may be. I ask Him for strength to accept anything He allows whether it be positive or negative. He is worthy of my praise for being God and for giving me life. I started noticing these daily blessings when I started praying His will. Things that I did not even ask Him for. As you will see, some things I thought about and others were just surprises. I am going to limit the blessings to the last two years after I totally surrendered to Him.

The First Airbnb

I wanted to rent out my house in Hampton, VA but I still wanted to be able to enjoy it myself. The house in Hampton reminds me of the summer home we had in Ocean Pines, MD. Ocean Pines is 20 minutes away from Ocean City, MD and Hampton is 35 minutes away from Virginia Beach, MD. There were nearby canals in Ocean Pines. There are nearby bodies of water in Hampton. The waterfront with benches to sit on is less than a mile from the house, and a stream and a small beach ten minutes away. First, let me tell you how the house in Hampton, VA came to be and then how it ended up being the desire of my heart.

My first husband Douglas was in the Airforce and he used his VA loan to purchase and have our house built in 1993 for $70,000. It is a rancher with an attached garage, three bedrooms, two full baths, a fireplace and a patio out back. When I was married to him, I did not know what I know now. When we hit a rough patch in our marriage, I could not handle it. We were arguing a lot and I did not want that for my children, so I moved out of our new home with the children, and we went to a shelter. I knew we were headed towards separation when we bought the house. We were living in base housing and would have to leave if not a family any longer.

Before I left, he told me that he did not want to lose the house. I told him if he did not fight me for the kids, he could have the house. I kept my word. I even helped him to keep it three times over the years by signing a refinance loan and two modification loans to lower his payments. We had a good relationship back then because he was always a good provider to the kids and me. I believe he became resentful of me after the child support converted to me receiving a third of his retirement. That is what the Air Force said I was entitled to because we had been married for 10 years. Well, for whatever reason, he stopped paying the mortgage and the house was going to go into foreclosure. My name was on the loan. My excellent credit took a dive to 525.

I would have had to pay taxes on the foreclosure. I saw God's blessing in a 700.00 check that came with both Douglas and my names on it. God told me to give it all to him and ask if he would sign a quit claim deed so I could take over the house. He agreed. We met at a notary. He signed it and I gave him the signed check. When we came outside, I went to give him a hug like I always had done, and he backed away from me and said that too much had happened. I do not understand what he meant to this day. I went to Hampton and told his tenant to now pay me the rent. After that tenant, I had two more tenants that turned out to be difficult for me. My friend Tamara told me that I should make it an Airbnb. I listened to her and in my mind, I was thinking, how could I afford to furnish an entire house to rent out

Once I retired under disability and surrendered to God. He opened an opportunity for me to have my heart's desire and be able to enjoy the house on occasion and earn income too. I used my lump sum from my social security to furnish the house in Hampton. I did it with God's help ordering everything from Amazon so I would not have to move any furniture. I even had the kitchen set and bedroom dresser assembled by Amazon.

As far as the decorating, God put it on my best friend Jean's heart to help me. Jean is an expert curtain hanger and has a good eye for decorating. We found beautiful bedspreads and curtains at the Goodwill store along with paintings. Jean stuck with me for days and dressed every window in the house and helped me brainstorm to make sure I had everything someone would need on a stay. I supply everything a hotel would supply like coffee, non-dairy creamer, sugar, pots and pans, plates, glasses, small appliances, detergent, shower gel, hand soap, trash bags, dishwasher detergent, shampoo, conditioner, blow dryer, razors, toothpaste and toothbrushes and candies. Most of these things, I purchased from the Dollar Tree. I took pictures and set up my Airbnb site on my cell phone. "The Peaceful Escape." Within six months, I was classified as a Superhost because of my excellent reviews!

God blessed the works of my hands. Jean introduced me to her friend Annie who has been my housekeeper for two years now. Annie is excellent. She does not miss a thing. She videocalls me after the clients leave, so that I can see how they left my house. That way I can leave an appropriate review. I pray for all my Airbnb clients, past, present and future and I have not had any real problems. They want to receive good reviews as well as I do. One of my first guests who I called my Angel, named Reginald, left me a box of chocolates. I drove from Baltimore so I could clean before I hired Annie and I stayed with Jean. I had just found out that my next-door neighbour Fred, had died.

Cracks in the Potter's Clay

I was feeling sad when I walked through the door and immediately felt the presence of the Holy Spirit. When I went into the kitchen, I saw the chocolates and just began to weep tears of joy instead of sadness. It made me feel as if I was not alone. He also left me a message to call his uncle, Garrett if I needed a handyman. Garrett has also been a blessing to me as a handyman for two years. God always puts a ram in the thicket. If you never heard that expression before, it is based on the Bible story about Abraham at the point of sacrificing his only son Isaac because God told him to and before he lowered the knife, God called out to him and told him to not lay a hand on the boy but to sacrifice the nearby lamb that had gotten stuck in the thicket bush.

Doris to the Rescue

Two years ago, was the lowest point in my life. I was alienated from all my immediate family. I was feeling unloved due to several reasons I will not go into. It is testifying time. I was suffering with a migraine. My marriage was in shambles and I felt alone. I was in the bed crying and I could not stop. It was making my head hurt even worse. I remember calling on the Lord in prayer. I began pleading with Him to just take me home. I was weeping hysterically and telling God that I wanted to go home and be with Him, that I did not want to keep living. Instead, I was ready to see Him and see my mother. As I was crying and feeling horrible, the phone beeped that I had a message.

I wiped my eyes to look at the phone and see who sent me a message. Doris? She usually posts in the morning. Well, she had sent me a song instead of a Bible reading. I could not believe my eyes. The song was called, "You Can't Die Yet". I knew it was from God, so I have never wanted to be dead since. I called Doris and asked her what she was doing when she sent me that song and she said that she was sitting on the edge of the bed thinking about me. Amazing. Glory to Yah.

Airbnb Number 2

While in my prayer closet crying that my children were not a part of my life, I decided to focus my attention on leaving them an inheritance. I wanted to be dead anyway, so I began preparing to go home to be with the Father. My mother left the house I grew up in and my sister no matter what our behaviour was. The house was a blessing to me, but it was old, and the basement still flooded. I decided to get the basement waterproofed. I had already turned the house in Hampton, VA into an Airbnb so I had a lawyer draw up a new deed with both my children's names on it. I added their names to inherit the house in Baltimore, MD in my will until after Andre and I divorced. He agreed to sign a quit claim deed to give me the house back after the divorce was final.

I then decided to turn the basement into an Airbnb. Jameliah Young is the leader of the Car Chronicles Movement on Facebook and she comes on live every day at 7:30am. She is indeed a prophetess and I believe the word she spoke that if you built during this pandemic season, God would make it prosper. I relied on my one year of architecture in college to design and drew a plan for the basement. My cousin Judy referred her handyman to me in the beginning of March 2020. We began work March 13th and finished the one-bedroom apartment in May. I say we because I assisted in the job. I am very handy with tools and wood. I took wood shop when I attended Baltimore Polytechnic High School. Being an artist, I am good with my hands and I have a lot of energy.

Unfortunately, being separated from my husband of 20 years, I was used to being a couple and I began to try to make relationships which God intended to meet certain needs in my life, into personal relationships that could lead to marriage. I was indeed moving too fast. My divorce was not even final, and I was planning my next husband. I was so close to God and desired His will, that I could not even consider having a casual affair. My licensed therapist, who is also an ordained minister, told me that she felt that Satan was tormenting me with men by having me think that every man that enters my life could be The One. I do not take medicine anymore, so I do not need a psychiatrist, but I still need a therapist. Les Brown always says that you cannot see the frame if you are in the picture.

Faded Pink Aluminium Siding, Fallen Branches and Writing Coach

One Sunday in November, I was walking up my sidewalk to the home I grew up in and I looked at the faded pink aluminium siding. I thought to myself; "I wonder if I could paint my siding because I know I don't have the money to get new siding." I dismissed the thought and focused on being grateful for my house even though it had faded. My mother bought two pink houses when she got home from NYU with her double masters. She brought a pink house for herself and a pink house 10 minutes away for her parents. My grandparents' house was a deep pink and ours was a pale pink. A few days after I had these thoughts, my Ring doorbell rang, and my dog Nikita started barking loudly as usual. I had just finished doing my YouTube devotion.

It was a contracting company notifying me that I had hail damage to my aluminium siding, and it was possible for my insurance company to cover its' replacement. The first insurance adjuster came out and did not find damage, but the contractor said that the adjuster probably did not use a flashlight in order to see the damage and to not be alarmed. The next insurance adjuster came and indeed found hail damage. 9,925,.00 was deposited into my account that evening and the remaining 10,000.00 will be deposited when the siding is completed in mid-April. A few days prior, several large tree branches had fallen in my backyard. On my morning run, I ran past some contractors cutting down a neighbour's tree. They agreed to walk to my house in order to give me an estimate. They charged me 700.00 to remove the branches.

I wanted to find an estimate under 20,000.00 because I had scheduled a meeting to speak with a writing coach in a few days and I knew I did not have money to pay for any services. In my mind, I wanted to have 1500.00 left over to pay for help with my book. I went to my neighbours' who had recently had their siding replaced and got the name of their contractor and left him a message. I was planning on going to Home Depot to get an estimate from contractors who await work on the parking lot. Before I reached the men standing outside of Home Depot, the contractor called me, and I pulled over and answered the phone.

The contractor asked if my home was the same size as my neighbours and I told him that it was. He first gave me an estimate of 20,000. I did not say anything but was thinking that that was the same amount as the first contractor and then he just lowered his estimate so that I would have exactly 1500.00 writing budget left over. I did not ask him to lower the estimate. God was at work. When the contractor came to the house, we found out that we shared summer memories in that his family also had a home in Ocean Pines, MD. This gentleman had such a sweet spirit and at the conclusion of our contract signing, he offered to pray for the new president and vice-president of the United States. It was so nice to have someone initiate prayer considering I pray so much every day.

I had started writing my book, but I had never written a book before and had watched a free webinar. The author and writing coach called me one day while I was in my prayer closet. I did not recognize the number, but I answered the phone anyway. He introduced himself and we scheduled a zoom meeting for the upcoming Wednesday. When we met, I told him my budget and he agreed to design a program especially for me as his programs were five-month programs for considerably more money. He sent me google documents with valuable writing tips and we spent three hours on a zoom call developing my outline. He knew all the right questions to ask. He told me that I would need to come up with additional funding for publishing. I thought to myself; "God will provide."

God's Provision for My Book

One of the conditions of the contract I signed for the aluminium siding company was that I pay 199.00 to have it power washed by a company that they recommended. Money was coming in through my Airbnb's and I had enough for that. On the day of the treatment, I had jogged to the post office to mail one of my mosaic frames to someone and had done my Prayer Run on Facebook live. It was a struggle that day, but I pushed through it. God sensed my loneliness, and He touched my uncle's heart to call me. I was so happy to hear his voice and I was able to share with him what was on my mind. He gave me excellent Godly advice. I received a call from a strange number, but I answered it anyway.

It was the power wash technician. He said he was at my home. I told him I was minutes away at the post office. He called again and I told him that I was less than 200 yards, and I would jog. He told me not to jog. It was fine. I did not realize I needed to be at the house, or I would not have gone to the post office. He needed me to close the window where my air conditioner was and my front door. I had the storm door locked and door open because my dog Nikita likes to look out the door when I am away. He told me that the chemicals from power washing could get into the house. I had on my hoodie that I call my Holy Ghost SuperHero Costume. My friend Edward gave it to me.

It has a big cross on the front of it. Within the cross is the face of a lion with its beautiful, penetrating eyes as the focal point. It also has crosses on the sleeves and on the back a list of things that Jesus is. Very cool. I like to wear it when I videotape my Prayer Runs. As I approached my house, I saw a man walking from his truck with a huge smile on his face that put my mind at ease that I did not take too long. His name was Todd. He explained in detail the power wash process and began his work. I went inside. When he finished, he called me to let me know. I went out on the porch and he was standing at the foot of my steps. He told me that he liked my shirt.

I looked down at my red cross shirt I got from donating blood and he said, "Not that one. The one with the lion on it. Where did you get that? I need it." I told him a friend gave it to me and I would find out for him. Something about the way he said: "I need that." made me feel he was talking about more than the shirt. I asked him if he wanted me to pray for him. He seemed so relieved and said: "Would you really?". I invited him on the porch, faced him and took both of his hands and started praying for him. The Holy Spirit really led me in the prayer because when I was done praying tears were streaming down Todd's face. I went and got him some tissues from the kitchen and gave him a hug.

I told him that I send out inspirational videos every day and asked if he wanted me to send them to him and he said that he did. I also told him that I was writing a book and told him the title. He looked at me strangely and told me that he was Bipolar too and his loved ones were trying to convince him to get on medication. Wow. Talk about divine meetings. He asked me when I had finished my book could he buy a copy and have me sign it. I told him that I would. He then told me that he appreciated the prayer so much and wanted to thank me. He told me that he would pay for my power washing to show his gratitude. I was blown away. That was not the only way Todd was going to bless me.

I began sending him my devotions that day. I send out two videos per day to my loved ones and many of my contacts because I post at random times. God just led me to send my videos to people who have not even asked me to send them. It was hard in the beginning because I did not know if people wanted me to or not. Some people commented that they uplift them, but some people have never responded. I am very transparent in my videos and I let the Holy Spirit lead me on what to say. I never know what I am going to say. I just trust God and He provides the words. One day I shared that I was filing chapter 13 bankruptcy because of a bad decision I made in trusting someone that I thought was going to be my husband.

Todd called me that evening and said that he had spoken to a friend about me, and they really believed in my book. He said that he listened to my video and knew because of the chapter 13 bankruptcy, I may not have money to buy my books. He said that when it was time to publish my book to give my publisher his number so that he could pay for my first hardcover order. He said that he and his friend wanted to remain anonymous. I wept tears of joy. It was amazing to me that all I did was pray for Todd. What a blessing to come from a prayer. We are now friends, and I asked his permission to use his name because this book is also designed to show my appreciation to people. I want to give people their flowers while they are alive to smell them.

The Faulty Electricity

I had only been in Phoenix a few days when the guests at my Airbnb started texting me that the lights were flickering and that the furnace was not working at my Baltimore Airbnb. They were cold. A friend of mine took a kerosene heater for them to use. My electrician was able to look, but he told me the wires were old and needed to be replaced but that he could not do it due to his full-time job. A friend recommended me to a 24hr electrician in Maryland. I spent a lot of money on the road traveling and only had 350.00 in the bank. The initial work the electrician did in order to establish safety was 300.00. He worked until after 12:00am. I paid him that night and the next day he confirmed what my electrician Adrian had told me. The wires needed to be replaced and it would cost 1600.00.

I called the company back and told them to not let the electrician come back because I did not have the money. I had just filed bankruptcy and knew I would not qualify for credit. They said that they would get him to call me to talk about a payment plan. He was so sweet. He said if you need to pay biweekly, that is fine. If you need to pay monthly, that is fine. If you need three months to pay, that is fine. If you need six months to pay, that is fine. If you need 25 years to pay, that is fine. I was almost in tears. I called him my angel and added him and his son who worked with him to my prayer list. They did a wonderful job. No more lights flickering. I am so grateful, and I will be paying them in six months. God provides.

The Car Seat

It was my second week watching my angelic granddaughter, Kameha. She is a joy to watch. I watch her Mondays, Wednesdays and Fridays from 8:00 am to 3:00 pm. I love the hours. (Desire of my heart) They remind me of teaching hours. I taught those hours for 22 years. As I was driving to Christina and Charlie's place, I thought about asking her to leave me the car seat in case of an emergency. Well, I got so excited seeing Kameha break out in this huge smile when she saw me through the window, that I forgot to ask. I did not think any more about the car seat until after I went home, fed Nikita, and decided to take out the trash. When I got to the dump, I noticed a nice Graco car seat sitting on the ground next to the dump. It was in great shape. I stared at it for a minute and thought. If it were something wrong with it, the people would have thrown it inside the dump and not set it beside it. (Desire of my heart) Marion told me that I could take the cover off and wash it which I did and sanitized the entire chair.

The next day next to the dump was a child's electrical car. It will fit Kameha perfectly and she can ride it when she comes to visit me. I only must find an adapter to charge it. Once again, if it were trash, it would have been placed inside the dump. I sanitized it. I joke with a friend that I wonder what would be out there the next day. Well, the third day someone had put a can of vegetarian chili on the side of the dump. I laughed out loud because I do not eat meat anymore. Lol. I did not take the chili though because I do not eat canned foods anymore either. It was a fun three days. God grants us the desires of our hearts when we delight ourselves in Him and He gives us things that we do not know we desire until we get them. Three days later, on my prayer run, I found a walker exactly like the one Kameha has. When Kameha is a little older, she will already have toys to play with at grandma's house and a car seat in grandma's car.

The Third Airbnb

Before I left Baltimore, I put a lock on my bedroom door. It was the desire of my heart to rent out the top two bedrooms and leave my bedroom for me whenever I came back to visit. When I left Baltimore, my dear friend Marion was kind enough to come to the house and give the cats soft food and water. I thought to myself, "How can I rent this out under Airbnb with the cats?" Well, nothing is too hard for God. A dear healthcare provider who had stayed in the basement Airbnb called me while I was attending a workshop in Phoenix to see my Results Coach Jon Talarico present. She was uneasy staying in the house by herself but really needed a place to stay. I asked her if she liked cats and she said that she was fine with cats. I gave her a 50 percent discount per night. She will be there until the end of May. Amazing.

Cracks in the Potter's Clay

Your Children Will Return to Their Own Land

Jeremiah 31:15-17 This is what the Lord says: A voice is heard in Ramah, mourning and great weeping. Rachel weeping for her children and refusing to be comforted because her children are no more. This is what the Lord says: Restrain your voice from weeping and your eyes from tears, for your work will be rewarded, declares the Lord. They will return from the land of the enemy. So, there is hope for your future, declares the Lord. Your children will return to their own land.

My relationships with my children are restored and I am so grateful. God blessed my daughter to get pregnant with my granddaughter Kameha with Kameha's dad Charlie. Kameha was the bridge that allowed my daughter and I to find our way back to each other to begin to heal. Christina and Charlie wanted to share their new bundle of joy with family and friends in Baltimore, MD so they booked a weeklong trip to come to Baltimore to stay in August of 2020. While estranged from both of my children, I focused all my energy on leaving them a legacy and built the one-bedroom apartment Airbnb in the basement of my home. I asked Christina if they wanted to stay there and she told me that they were going to stay in a hotel near

Washington, DC between my house and her grandmother's house.

I was disappointed but I was so grateful that I would be seeing her and my granddaughter again, I did not push the issue. I was careful to respect her boundaries. My desire was for them to stay in the Airbnb for their visit. I told her that I would block the days off in case she changed her mind, but she told me that she did not want me to miss out on any money and to keep the days open. At first, I unblocked them, but the Holy Ghost told me to block them again which I did. It was a couple weeks before they were to arrive, and I received a phone call from Christina telling me of an unforeseen expense and asking if the Airbnb was still available. I said that it was. I stayed cool until I got off the phone and then I proceeded to jump up and down and scream: "Thank you Jesus!"

Joshua had been working through some issues he had with me which I think were compounded by the company he was keeping. I was falsely accused of something horrific. I admit that it did hurt my feelings. I will not even disclose it here. I spoke my truth and let it go. I realized the spiritual attack and decided to pray about it. It is on page 25 of my prayer book which can be found at the back of this book. I wrote: "Thank you for restoring and renewing my relationship with my son by the time I go to visit Kameha for her first birthday." Since I had already moved to Phoenix to help Christina and Charlie with Kameha, I began reading it differently. I said: "Thank you for restoring and renewing my relationship with my son by Kameha's first birthday." I read that for about a week.

March 26, 2021, I received a phone call from Joshua at 10:46 pm. I was icing Kameha's birthday cake at the time. I walked in the bedroom to get the phone. I get very few phone calls. He asked me if he could stop by for a few minutes. I asked him if he was alone, and he told me that he was and that he just wanted to take a quick nap. I figured he was driving Lyft and was tired. I told him: "Of course." He got to the house a little after 11:00 pm. He greeted me with a warm hug and lovingly played with Nikita. I had made the couch up for him and offered him something to eat but he had just eaten.

We spoke for a few moments about Kameha and the video I sent him of me telling Les Brown my story. I then asked him if the music was too loud. I was listening to Danny Gokey (gospel artist) music. He said that it was not and that he could sleep through anything. He took a nap and then knocked on my bedroom door to let me know that he was leaving. He left a little after 12:00. I looked at the clock and proceeded to praise Yahweh for being faithful to his word. God amazed me by answering that specific request. Habakkuk 2 says to write it down and make it plain so that a herald may run with it. The heralds are our angels. Whatever you want to happen in your life, write it down with the expected outcome by the expected date.

Nikita Healed from Epilepsy

Jeremiah 32:27 Behold, I am the Lord, the God of all flesh. Nikita is my four-year-old German Shepherd. When she turned two, she had her first seizure. I did not know what to do so I started stroking her and pleading the blood of Jesus over her. Her neck was stretched and contorted sideways. Her legs were all stiff and her body was shaking violently. I was so afraid. I was crying. My other German Shepherd was sitting next to her when it began, and he stood up and watched on in concern. When she began to settle down, she bit both my hands causing a few of my fingers to bleed.

I took her to the vet and learned that she was discombobulated and afraid and did not realize what she was doing when she bit me. At the time,

Cracks in the Potter's Clay

Andre and I were separated, and he wasn't able to take one of the dogs with him. I was alone with two big dogs who pulled me to the ground on one occasion, pulled me down the stairs on another and ran through me simultaneously taking my feet from under me and causing me to fall flat on the ground. Kinda like Dino used to do to Fred on the Flintstones. I spent time in physical therapy for my back and neck due to these falls.

I met Alvester, who was somewhat of a self-acclaimed dog trainer who had given me his number stating that he could help me with Kato. Al is also a Master Herbalist and Martial Artist. I was married at the time and Al became like a big brother to me. He worked with me and helped me so much with the dogs. I was doing well with them but I thought the seizures would be too much for me to handle. At the time, I was very isolated and depressed.

Bipolar people are very impulsive. My impulse was to post an ad on the SPCA website and Facebook to give Nikita away. I explained that she had epilepsy and that she would be free to a good home. An old acquaintance responded to the Facebook post. He had a dog and wanted another dog to keep company with the first. I told him that I had scheduled Nikita to be spayed in a week and that I would bring her there on a trial basis to see how it worked for that week, come back and get her spayed and bring her back after she was healed. I did not want anyone making Nikita a puppy factory. She stayed with them for the week without incident. Meanwhile, I had begun buying wine and drinking it in the house. Normally, I would have wine only while out dining.

I was depressed. I hardly ate and barely washed. I got an intriguing email from a woman named Alexandra Gross. Gross was my maiden name. Alexandra explained that she was looking for a friend for life to run with. She especially wanted a Shepherd because of their athletic abilities. Well, being in the depressed state that I was in, I looked at Kato and decided to see if she wanted him. Kato was off the chain because Andre discouraged me from socializing him as a puppy because he wanted a watchdog. We had a bad experience, and our previous dog did not do his job. Well, Kato had bitten my neighbour because he hugged my son Joshua and he saw it as a threat. He bit my stepdaughter Morgan because she just walked in the house unexpectedly. He tried to bite my stepson, Eric who had stopped over for a rare visit, but Eric was too fast for him. He pulled a chair in between them. Do not get me wrong. I absolutely adored Kato. He reminded me of my old dog

Cracks in the Potter's Clay

Sampson who was a tan lab/chow mix. He was a huge, gentle, intelligent dog.

I thought Kato had Sampson's spirit because of the way he looked at me and the way he turned around in the bathtub for me when I gave him a bath. Just like Sampson, Kato turned around in the tub so I could wash the other side of him. He also waited to shake until I pulled the shower curtain closed and told him to shake. Alexandra was alone and I thought Kato would be a good watch dog for her. I am a black belt in Kenpo with a bad temper. I have an advantage as a woman alone. Like Mr. T would say: "I pity the fool...that messes with me." I did not have much to give, and I really was ready to check out of this thing called life anyway. I was ready to be alone, so I told her to come and meet Kato. They fell in love immediately.

She spent about an hour at the house with us and when I started putting his things in her car, he began barking as he was tied on a leash in the front yard. Her back car door was open. I unattached Kato from the leash and he ran and jumped into her car! Two home visits later, Kato was running five miles with Alexandra, running across her land searching for his food that she hides from him, climbing mountains and swimming in streams. They were destined to be together. Giving Kato away was one of the most unselfish things that I had ever done. I really did love him, but I was not loving myself at the time. My mother and my friend, Harold Cornish commented on my Facebook post that it was a real life "Sophie's Choice." I had to watch the movie to understand what he meant. It really was.

I got Nikita back and she was spayed. Two weeks passed and she had healed well. I was in a major depression and did not even want to take care of myself. I reached out to the acquaintance and told him that I was having a hard time mentally and asked if he could pick up Nikita instead of me making the 45-minute drive again. He said that he would. I had packed all her things, including her shot record and I waited and waited and waited. I did not receive a text message, or a phone call the day that he was supposed to pick her up. That told me a lot. To me, that was irresponsible. I thought that if he could not even come and pick her up, he would not be a good owner for my dog. I told him that I was keeping my dog.

Five o'clock the next morning, Nikita had her second seizure. She was asleep in the bed with me. I jumped up and ran out of the room and shut her inside to prevent my getting bitten again. I had to wait for the seizure to stop and then for her to stop pacing the floor disoriented for another 20 minutes before I could go get her and give her a bath. I also had to clean the sheets and floor because she would urinate and defecate during the seizures. The vet prescribed phenobarbital for her. Despite taking the medicine, she continued to have a seizure every week at five o'clock in the morning. The medicine clearly was not working. I was off medicine and I really did not want her on it.

I called Alvester, who is also an herbalist. I asked him if he could make some herbs to help Nikita and he told me that he would. Al delivered the herbs for Nikita and I started her on them. He told me how to give it to her with the phenobarbital and how to wean her off it. When the herbs got down to half of the 4 oz jar, I called Al so that he could make her some more. She was not taking the phenobarbital any longer and I did not want her to run out. Al did not answer the phone and what was more surprising, he did not call me back.

About two weeks later, I decided to call Al because he had told me that he was treating himself for a condition. I wanted to know how he was doing. When he told me that he had made a successful remedy with the herbs, I began to weep and praise the Lord. We are dear friends. He then asked me how Nikita was doing. I had not even realized that she had not had a seizure since she started taking the herbs that he made for her. Al then began to celebrate. He confessed that he did not answer the phone for me on purpose when I called. He said that he put his heart into making the right mixture of herbs for Nikita and even prayed over the herbs that they would work. He knew I was separated with not much money and he did not want me to have an added expense buying herbs for Nikita more than once.

That was two years ago. Nikita turns four on Easter tomorrow. It is April 3, 2021. Nikita is a big part of my healing and ministry. You see, God told me to run every day to combat insomnia and mood swings. He told me three or four days of exercise is not enough for me. I began running a mile a day and praying for people on Facebook Live while I run. God told me to begin praying for people and encourage them to exercise. He told me to let them know when I do not feel like running but show them that I am doing it anyway. I feel that if I can do it, anyone can do it. I demonstrate a disciplined life and love to inspire others to do the same.

The big blessing about Nikita is that although God requires me to do my daily Devotion on Youtube and daily Facebook Prayer Run. He does not hold me to a specific time. He does not because it takes me time to get my body, mind and spirit right before I can represent Him. I must reach a certain level of worship before I try to encourage others. Sometimes it is night-time before I do my prayer run. Because Nikita is so big and strong, 90 lbs., no one bothers us. In fact, they cross the street when they see us coming. Yes. Nikita is my gift from God. Since she had neurological problems too, I say that we are each other's service animals. The runs are the highlight of her day.

Car Story Update

Remember the story of my smoker friend that stole my car? Well, a week later my car was found parked, undamaged and in the back seat on the floor was my pocketbook with all of my credit cards, ID's and money inside. Praise the Lord.

Conclusion

I have written this book as a tool to encourage others with Bipolar I, that it is possible to live a productive life without the use of medication. The keys to my success are:

1. Have a daily prayer routine that includes affirmations of what you desire that you do

consistently without fail. If you are alive, wake up and give thanks.

2. Do a detox and eat only those things that are good for you. Drink plenty of water daily, get sunlight and build your immune system in order to prevent catching viruses.

3. Walk in the truth. Be honest or choose not to answer. God knows everything so do not worry about what people think or say. Only worry about the judgement of the Creator. There is great freedom in walking in the truth.

4. Exercise daily. This will enable you to sleep better and improve your mood. Remember, we have an excess of energy to burn off. Use the energy wisely and intentionally. Write a list of things to accomplish every day and check them off as you go along. It will give you a sense of accomplishment and pride. Productive people are happy people.

5. Watch what negative information you allow into your mind and space. Seek to only speak positive about yourself and others. If you do not have anything kind to say, do not say anything at all. Change the subject if someone is talking negatively or excuse yourself.

6. As my mentor Les Brown suggests: Hang around OQP-only quality people. Associate

with like-minded individuals going in the direction that you are.

7. Love God and love yourself first. The Bible says to love the Lord your God with all your heart and with all your soul and to love your neighbour as yourself. I had to learn that loving yourself is a prerequisite for loving others.

8. Believe in God. Believe in yourself and never give up. Delight yourself in the Lord and He will give you the desires of your heart. **Psalm 37:4**

Mark 11:23-24 For verily I say unto you, that whosoever shall say unto this mountain, be thou removed, and be thou cast into the sea and shall not doubt in his heart but shall believe that those things which he saith shall come to pass he shall have whatsoever he saith.

The most important takeaway from my book is to have a personal relationship with God and trust Him with your life.

CONTACT THE AUTHOR

Where you can find me:

Email: Trustgod@allisonjoan.com
Website: Allisonjoan.com
Youtube: @Allison Joan Hall
Facebook: @Allison Joan Hall
Instagram: @Allisonjoan4566

Dances on Youtube in order of performance:

Type in the search bar; Allison Joan Hall followed by each:

1. ....Hills and Valleys, Tauren Wells
2. ....My Worship is For Real. Bishop Larry D. Trotter
3. ....Known.,Tauren Wells
4. ....God's Not Done With You, Tauren Wells
5. ....Encourage Yourself, Donald Lawrence
6. ....Wanted, Danny Gokey Dance-Liturgical Dance 53 year old
6. ....Wanted, Danny Gokey Dance-Liturgical Dance 53 Pt 2
7. ....Fix Me Jesus, Revelations

My mother was a great influence in my life. I watched her perform this skit numerous times. I do it exactly like she did.
Youtube: Allison Joan Hall
It's Showdown Time Excerpt - My Dance Video Allison Joan Hall

Finally, on Youtube: I presented my story to Les Brown tonight! Glory to God.

Master Herbalist:
Alvester Jacobs III
aborigin_al@icloud.com

Audio Recording:
Cosmic Soup Recording
www.cosmicsouprecording.com

Optional Reading

Prayer Book

This section is not a part of the book but for me, it helped make the book possible. This is the 25-page loose leaf binder with prayers written on notebook paper that I read every day before I leave the house. Most of the scriptures have already been referenced in the book. I am including this as a testament to all the people that I told I was adding them to my prayer book. I really did! This book may help people who do not know how to talk to God and get results. You do not need a computer to write your prayers down. Unfortunately, once scanned, it would be too small to read so I typed it. I always write my prayers by hand. Now, I laminate the pages to last longer. As God answers prayers, I revise. God bless you.

Prayer Book

Habakkuk 2:2

Then the Lord replied: Write down the revelation and make it plain on tablets so that a herald may run with it.

Cracks in the Potter's Clay

Galatians 5:22-23

Fruit of the Spirit in the life of the believer are: love, joy, peace, patience, kindness, goodness, gentleness, faithfulness and self-control.

Romans 12:18

If it is possible as far as it depends on you, live at peace with everyone.

James 4:8

Draw near to God and He will draw near to you.

John 10:27

My sheep listen to my voice, I know them and they follow me.

Proverbs 16:20

Whoever gives heed to instruction prospers and blessed is the one who trusts in the Lord.

Hebrews 10:25

Not giving up meeting together as some are in the habit of doing but encouraging one another and all the more as you see the day approaching.

Joshua 1:8

Study this book of instruction continually. Meditate on it day and night so you will be sure to obey everything written in it. Only then will you prosper and succeed in all you do.

1 Peter 5:8

Be alert and of sober minds. Your enemy the devil prowls around like a roaring lion looking for someone to devour.

Psalm 138:7

Though I walk in the midst of trouble, thou will revive me; thou shalt stretch forth thine hand against the wrath of mine enemies, and thy right hand shall save me.

Cracks in the Potter's Clay

Isaiah 26:3

Thou wilt keep him in perfect peace whose mind is stayed on thee because he trusteth in thee.

James 1:19

Wherefore my beloved brethren, let every man be swift to hear, slow to speak, slow to wrath.

James 4:7

Submit yourselves therefore to God, resist the devil and he will flee from you.

Isaiah 54:13

All of my children will be taught of the Lord and great will be the peace between them.

Isaiah 54:17

No weapon formed against me shall prosper and I will refute every tongue that accuses me.

Psalm 139:23-24

Search me oh God and know my heart, try me and know my thoughts and see if there be any wicked way in me and lead me in the way everlasting.

Proverbs 14:7

A quick-tempered man acts foolishly, and a man of wicked intentions is hated.

Proverbs 16:32

He who is slow to anger is better than the mighty and he that rules his spirit than he who takes a city.

Proverbs 17:27

He who has knowledge spares his words and a man of understanding is of a calm spirit.

Mark 11:23-24

For verily I say unto you that whosoever shall say unto this mountain, be though removed, and be thou cast into the sea and shall not doubt in his heart but shall believe that those things which he saith shall come to pass, he shall have whatsoever he saith.

Cracks in the Potter's Clay

Mathew 12:50 For whosoever shall do the will of my Father which is in heaven the same is my brother and sister and mother.

Song of Solomon 2:14

O daughters of Jerusalem, I adjure you by the gazelles and does of the field: Do not arouse or awaken love until the time is right.

Job 22:28

What you decide will be done and light will shine on your ways.

James 4:7

If anyone then knows the good they ought to do and doesn't do it. It is sin for them.

Jeremiah 32:27

Behold, I am the Lord the God of all flesh. Is there anything to hard for me?

Mathew 16:19

I will give you the keys of the kingdom of heaven: whatever you bind on Earth will be bound in heaven, and whatever you loose on Earth will be loosed in Heaven.

Jeremiah 33:3

Call unto me and I will answer thee and show thee great and mighty things which thou knoweth not.

Thank you, Father, for waking me up clothed in my right mind with activity of my limbs and all my senses HaleluYah. Good morning Abba Father, Yahshua and Holy Spirit. Thank you for letting me see the sunshine again. Holy Spirit you are welcome in this place. Have your way in my life today.

Guide my thoughts, words and deeds. Thank you for not letting me get any bad news during the night and for giving me the strength to endure anything that you allow good or bad. I know that all things work together for good for those who love You and are called according to Your purpose.

Thank you for providing me with food, clothes, shelter, heat, running water, indoor bathrooms, beds to sleep on, and appliances. Please forgive me and my loved ones of our sins of omission and commission. Thank you for 1 John 1:9 If we confess our sins, You are faithful and just to forgive us our sins and cleanse us from all unrighteousness. Please continue to bless me and my loved one with divine health according to Isaiah 53:5 For He was wounded for our transgressions. He was bruised for our iniquities. The chastisement of our peace was upon Him and by His stripes we are healed. Thank you for Mathew 10:1 You gave Your disciples power against unclean spirits to cast them out and to heal all manner of sickness and all manner of diseases. Thank you for letting my granddaughter, Kameha have a bowel every day and keeping her healthy and safe from accidents and anyone who would do her harm. Thank You for Psalm 91:14 For the Lord says because He loves me, I will rescue him. I will make him great because he trusts in my name. Thank you for financial success from being a part of Les Brown's Power Voice Academy and Jon Talarico's Thinking Into Results courses.

Thank you for Psalm 9:15-16 When he calls on me, I will answer, I will be with him in trouble and rescue him and honor trouble and I will satisfy him with a full life and give him my salvation. Please provide all our needs according to Your riches in glory.

Philippians 4:19 Please motivate me and my loved ones to delight ourselves in you and you give us the desires of our hearts. Psalm 37:4 Help us to always accept what you allow and always be grateful to you for all you have done. Thank you for salvation. I will enter your gates with thanksgiving and enter your courts with praise. I will be thankful unto you and bless your name for you are good and your mercy is everlasting, and your truth endures forever. Your truth endures to all generations. Please deliver me and my loved ones from all strongholds, unforgiveness and bondage in the name of Jesus. Please let us live long happy, healthy lives that honor you. Please let our children outlive us and please let us all die peaceably. Please minister to Adrienne, Joshua, Ali, Douglas, Anisah, Layla, Christina, Kameha, Charlie, Macky, Charles, Uncle Buzzy, Theresa, RIcky, Crystal and family, Amina, Carmen, Sheila and Tamara. Please tell me when and how to use my gifts. Please use me and guide me in all that I think, say and do in Jesus' name. Please be glorified through me when I dance. Please continue to give me the moves through your Holy Spirit. Thank you for preserving and healing my body from the top of my head to the souls of my feet and all that is within me. Please order my steps in your Word. Please bless the relationships in my life and remove any you do not want there. Please continue to lead me to the physical activities you want me to do and the foods you want me to eat. Thank you for healing me from Bipolar 1 and setting me free. Thank you for healing _____ soul, body, mind and spirit and for setting _____ free from _____ and all _____. Thank you for setting _____ and_____ free from all _____. Thank you for keeping my children and loved ones healthy. Thank you for ordering your angels to protect me and my loved one. Thank you for healing Jordan and Trudi. Thank you for providing for me and my loved ones. Please reveal my sinful ways so that I can repent. Thank you for my successful Airbnb's that will enable me to pay off my houses before I die so my children can just enjoy the houses. Thank you for letting them be responsible for the houses and keep them up. Thank you for my contentment and for making me feel loved. I only want what you want for me Father. Thank you for saving my father, brothers, niece, nephews, stepmother, sister-in-laws and any other unsaved loved ones. Thank you for saving me and using me to bring others to you. Thank you for leading me to do kicks, leaps, turns and acrobatics when I dance in Your name and glorify you. Thank you for healing my spine, hives, skin, back, hand and migraines. I love you Yahweh my creator. Thank you for blessing me, Daddy, Cousin Edythe, Ronnie, Uncle Buzzy, Theresa, Trigger, Audrey, Deanna, Judy and their loved ones. Thank you for blessing and leading Joshua, Christina, Kameha, Charlie, Morgan, Jabre, Chase, Kisha, Logan, Danasia, Mikiyah, Paris, Journey, Jabrea, Ronea, Eric, Kenny, Charlie and their loved ones. Thank you for letting Christina live to raise her children and grandchildren. Thank you for blessing Joshua's seed and for his longevity. Thank you for using my children's gifts to glorify you. Thank you for blessing Adrienne, Amina, Joy, Omar, Hassan, Ali, Jasmine, Jackson, Charlotte and children. Anisah, Layla, Alayah, Isaiah, Kadijah, Jen, Jeb, Darnell, Kevin, Michael, Dwayne, Charles, Colleen, Charlene, Chavonne, Steve, Winston, Faye, Charlynn, Charles, Shaniah, Mike-Mike, Madison, Lil Kevin and family, Sheila and family, Tracey, Douglas, Jaliyah, Semone, Emeri, Herbert, Mary, Sue, Jenny, Clarence, Danny, Dean, Lottie and all their families, the Johnsons, the Grays, the MacMurray, Andre, LaShelle and Aji, the Smiths, Jean, Sheila, Alexis and Louis, Heather, Steve, Autumn, Ms. Robinson, Tony, Mr. Cooper, Howard, Henry, Waverly, Shy, Bro Nate, Doris and loved ones, Veda, Edward, Shirley, Colleen, Rosalin, Michelle, Cece, Yvonne, Marion, Joseph, Howard, Isabella, Gerl, Leon, Allison, Patrick, Daryl, David

Cracks in the Potter's Clay

Spruill, Carol, Erma, Kevin, Julian, Teresa, Cameil, Kailah, Michael, Dean, Janine, and families, Shabray, Alliner, Larry, Tiesha, Pattie, Yvette, Angie, Archie, Joyce, Rev. Batty, Rev. Marsha, Bro. Brown, Dolores, JoAnn, Bishop Kennedy and family and church family. Chris Johnson and family, Tim and Denise Pace, Tony from BGE, Rosie, Alberto, Destini, Kevin Knowlin and family, Delino, Gloria, Chaborra, Rochelle, Emma, Ernest, Bailey, Carol, Emmy, Ander, Becky, Brian and their girls. Doc, Pam, Marina, Wary, Oswoldo, Miluska, Silvia, Greg, Pastor MacAfee, Erica, Max, Peggy Wall, St. John AME church family, COGSOC, FCWC, New Creations church families. Maria, my Facebook family, FPKK family, my neighbors, old students and co-workers, Kalyan, Delphia, Sara, Jonathan, Deb, Jackie, Jason, Debra, Todd, Bryce, Elle Mauwsi, Faith, Dolcas, Shanell China, Sasha, Leandre, Nia, CSU Toastmasters, Lee Michaels, Peter Alaya, Earl, Andrea, Bob Proctor, Judy, Shlomo, Jessica, Daliesha, Monica, Paul, Ralph, Michael, Cheryl and families. Susan and family, Janet and family, Daya, Muhammad, Yashica, Latoya, Wendy, Hanna, Ali, Paulette and family, Rachel, Luke, Janine, Sawyer, Phyl, Grace, Mathew, Tarnisha, Bryan, Nan and Ed, Winnifred Wedderburn, CJ and Rick, Donalyn Reed, Janek, Andrew, Matt Aston, Eservere, Pastor Luke and wife and their relationship, Fernanda, Noel, Raquel, Novell, Pratibha, Karon Green, Cynthia,

Alvester, Rodney, Ryan, Pepperjack, Ben, Iyanna, George, Anthony, Falana, Nefra, Johnisha, Jessica and daughter, Shawntee, Frank, Shenise and mate, Alice, Ron, Sallie, Amy, Junie, Cyndee, Erica, Rico, Teresa, All of my Airbnb guests past, present, and future, Daniel, Victor Jr., Fatima, David, Paulette, Timothy, Katrina, Raphael, Seth, Seth Jr., Clarrie, Tony, Zynair, Rashad, Canon Aubrey Smith and his mom and dad, Teniecka, Karena, DeVante, Anisha, Malasha, Lori, Dave Arm, Karen, Kelechi, Latoya W., Nico, Tamala, Cynthia, Eunice, Shirley, Rosita, Mildred, Andre, Dannette, Marinda and family, Cousin Ann, Tricia, David, Dougie, Donna, Angelo, Latoya, James and families, Kathy, Jerome, Karen and family, Jay, Joe, Ralph, Dee-Dee, Cordelia, Leah, Ralph, Reggie, Bryon, Nataki, Rasheeda, Annette, Peggy, Thelma, Faith, Tyrone, Terry, Timmy, Mr. Smith, Tonese and family, Keith, Tonya, Penny, Robbie, Alec, BJ, Karen, Kirk, Lavinia, Teresa, Josette, Tory, Valerie, Deacon Tony, Monica, Charles and Alice Howard, Rose Dower, MIcah, Charlton, Darius, Justin, Jyleanna, Mr. Smith, Missy and families, Shirnette, Joyce Meyer, Creflo Dollar, Jimmy Swaggart, TD Jakes, Priscilla Shirer, Bishop McMillan, Dale Bronner, Karen Wheaton, TV Ministers, Facebook Ministers, the Pridgens, Evelyn, Sandra, Junius, Robin, Mary, Cheryl, Antoinette, Dexter, Chante Moore, Tanya, Les Brown and loved ones, Thelma Warton, Linda,

Cracks in the Potter's Clay

Robin C., Roselyn, Tommy, Ashley, Lily, Andrea, Michelle, Agnes, Rhona, Terri, Sherri, Flo, Hazel, Judy, Kevin, Shantrise, William, Rosaclarita, Pam, Sandi, Isis, Giselle, Giles, Kittrell, Renae, Nova, Joe, Alphonso, Lisa, Nicole, Eva, Christina, Adam, Brian, Al and Paul, Delores, Ronald, Dwane, Aisha, DIonna, Franklin, Toni, Kashanda, the Rogers, Becca and Jack, Alva, Gwen, Suzette, Cynthia, India, Jorge, Vanessa, Lorre, Marisol, John, Yvonne, Twila, Thaliya, Marlon, Troy, Connie and families John, Trina, Roberta Carter and grandson, Juanita, Trina, Jai, Carrisa and family, Claudia, Eva, Dirk, Kendra, Alison, Marcos, Tiky, Tamsen, Ron, Colleen, Deatrice, James, Pat, Anna, Marty, James, Ann, Lydia, Alica, Shantell, Sandra, Kathleen, Andrew, Eva, India, Domenika, Talia, Meghann, Mason, Delano, Raphael, Gary, Naomi, Aliria, Alesha, Gary, Macey, Carol, Vanessa, Casey, Sid, Power Voice Family, Eric Hamlin, Jon Talarico, JiLlian, Baby Jasper, Marcia, Oshain, Wayne, Troy, Yansen, Ella, Ellouise, Annie, Carolyn, Eddie, Josiah, Tamar, Genoh, Moni, Alex, Ava, Kennard, Karen, Annette, George, Jerry, Aramis, Athos, Dartanya, Lil Doc, Edith, Tim, Laverne, Elisabeth, Rosalyn, Eric, Leon, Dwight, Jessica, Josselin, Sherrie, Angel, Aaron, Lasandra, Celina, Lori, Anthony, Jonathan, Gabriel, Alicia, Cherelle and baby, Chenell, Andre, Edward and families, Ian, Ellis, Carla, Clifton and families, Roy Ayers and band, AJ Diamoncutter, Chanel

England and loved ones, William, Earl, Freda, Jermisha, Paula, June, Tracey, Dell and mom, Travis, Synyan, Rev Emma, Donna, Charlie, Yulanda, Garrett, Reginald, Lena, Rodney and Carleen, Lasse, Greg, Naisla, Andaiye, Aubrey, Kathleen, Marjarie, Eric, Quinn, Naomi, Emily, Brittney, Benjamin, Jeremy, Byron, Annie, Alexandra, MJ, Fred, Valerie, Ana, Brenda, Eileen and families, Kato, Nikita, Carey, Smokey, Goldie, Maurice, Calen Wynn, Taneisha, Lennwood and Coco, Michael and Cindy McCoy, Yuvisela, Simone, Ify, Precious and Leon, Rhonda Macky, Sabado, Carla, Carmello, J, Brownie, and Melissa Caudle.

Thank you for sending the right guests to the Peaceful Escape and the Secret Place. Thank you for letting the Corona virus pass over me and my loved ones. You are all powerful God. Thank you for blessing and healing Tim, Colleen, Erin and my Hampton neighbours. According to Isaiah 54:13 all my children will be taught of the Lord and great will be the peace between them. As in Ephesians 6:1-3 Let Joshua, Christina and Kameha honour their mother and father that thy days be long upon the earth and that it may go well with them. According to Prov 3:21-22 for my children Father preserve sound judgement and discernment do not let them out of their sight let them be life for them an ornament to grace their necks. 2 Cor 10:4 The weapons of our warfare are not carnal but mighty through God to the pulling down of strongholds in _____, _____, and _____lives and me and all my loved ones. Casting down imaginations and every high thing that exalts itself against the knowledge of God and bringing into captivity every thought to the obedience of Christ. In Jesus name. Thank you. You say in Luke 11:9-10. Teach us how to fight Father. Please let _____hair grow back and let_____ make her feel loved and appreciated. Bless Charlynn's life always Father. Please give her the desires of her heart for her faithfulness to her brother and sisters. Thank you for blessing Queen Esther's Estates and for Sheila retiring by November 1, 2021. Please do whatever you have to do to bring my loved ones and keep me in right fellowship with you Father. Bless Black men, women and children in the US and all people everywhere please. Thank you for giving me wisdom, guidance in all I do, patience, forgiveness, longsuffering, strength, understanding, discernment and for using me as you see fit. Bless my mind. I love you Yahweh my Creator, Yahshua my Savior and Holy Spirit, my Comforter. Father, please turn _____life around and let___ know that this is not the life you want_____ to be involved in. Thank you that_____, _____ and _____have rededicated their lives to you and are experiencing great freedom from all hinderances in Jesus' name Amen. Thank you for this word for_____ and _____Jeremiah 32:15-17 This is what the Lord says: A voice in heard in Ramah, mourning and great weeping. Rachel weeping and refusing to be comforted because her children are no more. This is what the Lord says: Refrain your voice from weeping and your eyes from tears, for your work will be rewarded declares the Lord. They will return from the land of the enemy. So, there is hope for your future declares the Lord. Your children will return to their own land. Isaiah 61:3 Thank you for giving me a garment of praise instead of a spirit of despair. Isaiah 61:7 Thank you that instead of shame my children will receive a double portion and instead of disgrace they will rejoice in their inheritance and so they will inherit a double portion in their land and everlasting joy will be theirs. Father, I believe your Word for_____Isaiah 57:18 You have seen____ways, but you will heal ___ anyway. Thank you for your promise in Isaiah 45:23 You have sworn by yourself the word is gone out of your mouth in righteousness and shall not return. That unto me every knee shall bow. Every tongue shall swear Prov 22:6 says train up a child in the way that he should go and when he is old, he will not depart from it. Isaiah 46:4 assures me that even to my old age and gray hairs. I am He, I am He who will sustain you. I have made you. I will carry you. I will sustain and I will rescue you. In the name of Jesus, I use His name, blood and word to pull down all strongholds, imaginations and lies in _____ and _____ mind. I destroy every obstacle, every wrong relationship and influence that is keeping _____ and _____from God. I pull down these rebellious thoughts and declare_____ and_____ will obey Christ. I claim 2 Cor 5:18-20 That I am an ambassador of Jesus. Help me not be anxious for anything. Father whatever your will is for my life, let It be done.

Goal Card

I am so happy and grateful now that I am making 7 million dollars or more a year by December 31, 2021 and that I am the most sought-after female African American motivational speaker, liturgical dancer, story teller, artist and singer in the world. Thank you that my and Sheila's books are both best sellers on Amazon, New York Times, USA Today and Internationally selling 70 million copies or more between us. Thank you that I am a guest of Steve Harvey, Joyce Meyer and that I dance to Danny Gokey singing live. Thank you that my Airbnb's are making me increasing money every year. Thank you for restoring and renewing my relationship with my son and for his successful book by October 8, 2021. My children call me blessed. All my loved ones will live long, happy, prosperous, healthy lives and die peacefully. I speak all these things in Jesus' name. Amen

Cracks in the Potter's Clay

Made in the USA
Middletown, DE
21 May 2021

39740606R00109